Confession of Faith

in a
Mennonite Perspective

Translations Available

Dutch	Amsterdam, Netherlands
French	Montbéliard, France
German	Winnipeg, Manitoba
Laotian	Winnipeg, Manitoba
Russian	Winnipeg, Manitoba
Spanish	Scottdale, Pennsylvania
Vietnamese	Winnipeg, Manitoba

Available Online

Complete text	www.mennolink.org/doc/cof
Summary Statement	www.mph.org/confess

Translations in Process

Japanese	Tokyo, Japan
Korean	Seoul, South Korea

Confession of Faith

in a
Mennonite Perspective

Published by arrangement with the General Board of
the General Conference Mennonite Church and the
Mennonite Church General Board

Continued authorization by the General Board of
Mennonite Church Canada and the Executive Board
of Mennonite Church USA

HERALD PRESS
Scottdale, Pennsylvania
Waterloo, Ontario

Library of Congress Cataloging-in-Publication Data
Confession of faith in Mennonite perspective.
    p. cm.
"Published by arrangement with the General Board of the General
 Conference Mennonite Church and the Mennonite Church General Board."
    ISBN 0-8361-9043-2 (pbk.)
    1. Mennonites—Creeds. 2. General Conference Mennonite Church—
Creeds. 3. Mennonite Church—Creeds. I. General Conference
Mennonite Church. II. Mennonite Church. III. Title.
BX8124.C66 1966
238'.973—dc20   95-43805

The paper used in this publication is recycled and meets the minimum
requirements of American National Standard for Information Sciences—
Permanence of Paper for Printed Library Materials, ANSI Z39.48-1984.

Unless otherwise indicated all Scripture quotations and references are from
the *New Revised Standard Version Bible* (NRSV), copyright © 1989, by the
Division of Christian Education of the National Council of the Churches of
Christ in the USA. Used by permission.

CONFESSION OF FAITH IN A MENNONITE PERSPECTIVE
Copyright © 1995 by Herald Press, Scottdale, Pa. 15683
    Published simultaneously in Canada by Herald Press,
    Waterloo, Ont. N2L 6H7. All rights reserved
Library of Congress Catalog Number: 95-43805
International Standard Book Number: 0-8361-9043-2
Printed in the United States of America
Book design by James M. Butti; cover symbol by Glenn Fretz
Cover design by Gwen M. Stamm

06 05 04   14 13 12 11

To order or request information, please call
1-800-759-4447 (individuals); 1-800-245-7894 (trade).
Website: www.mph.org

Table of Contents

Inter-Mennonite Confession of Faith Committee

Members who prepared and recommended this Confession of Faith to the General Boards were Marlin E. Miller (co-chair), S. David Garber, Beulah Hostetler, Samuel Lopez, and Ann Weber-Becker, representing the Mennonite Church; and Helmut Harder (co-chair), Lois Barrett, Heinz Janzen, Jake Tilitzky, and Ted VanderEnde, representing the General Conference Mennonite Church.

Introduction

Statements of what Mennonites believe have been among us from earliest beginnings. A group of Anabaptists, forerunners of Mennonites, wrote the Schleitheim Articles in 1527. Since then, Mennonite groups have produced numerous statements of faith. This *Confession of Faith in a Mennonite Perspective* takes its place in this rich confessional history. The historic creeds of the early Christian church, which were assumed as foundational for Mennonite confessions from the beginning, are basic to this confession as well.

This confession is the work of two Mennonite groups in North America, the Mennonite Church (MC) and the General Conference Mennonite Church (GC).

The Mennonite Church, organized in North America in 1898 by several regional conferences of Swiss-South German background, has recognized a number of confessions: the Schleitheim Articles (Switzerland, 1527), the Dordrecht Confession (Holland, 1632), the Christian Fundamentals (1921), and the Mennonite Confession of

Faith (1963). Later confessions have been adopted while still recognizing earlier documents.

The General Conference Mennonite Church was organized in 1860, when some groups with roots in the Mennonite Church joined with Swiss and German Mennonite groups who had more recently immigrated from Europe. Later, the General Conference added congregations of Dutch-Prussian descent. The lengthy Ris Confession (Holland, 1766) has been widely used in General Conference circles. Also widely used were various regional confessions and adaptations of the Elbing Confession (West Prussia, 1792). In 1896 the General Conference adopted the Common Confession and in 1941 approved a Statement of Faith for its new seminary.

How do Mennonite confessions of faith serve the church? First, they provide guidelines for the interpretation of Scripture. At the same time, the confession itself is subject to the authority of the Bible. Second, confessions of faith provide guidance for belief and practice. In this connection, a written statement should support but not replace the lived witness of faith. Third, confessions build a foundation for unity within and among churches. Fourth, confessions offer an outline for instructing new church members and for sharing information with inquirers. Fifth, confessions give an updated interpretation of belief and practice in the midst of changing times. And sixth, confessions help in discussing Mennonite belief and practice with other Christians and people of other faiths.

In its format, this confession follows some traditional patterns, but also introduces new elements in line with our Anabaptist heritage. As in the past, the confession is arranged as a series of articles. The Articles appear in four sets. The first eight Articles (1-8) deal with themes common to the faith of the wider Christian church. The second set (Articles 9-16) deals with the church and its practices, and the third set (Articles 17-23) with discipleship. The final article (24) is on the reign of God. Each article makes an important contribution to this confession of faith, regardless of its order here. In this confession, each article begins with a summary paragraph and is followed by a commentary. In addition, the topics of most articles are found in former confessions. But there are some new titles, such as "Christian Spirituality." Finally, as in former confessions, the articles are based on biblical texts. Scripture references are to the New Revised Standard Version (NRSV).

The *Confession of Faith in a Mennonite Perspective* was adopted at the delegate sessions of the General Conference Mennonite Church and the Mennonite Church, meeting at Wichita, Kansas, July 25-30, 1995. The twenty-four articles and summary statement were accepted by both groups as their statement of faith for teaching and nurture in the life of the church. The commentary sections were endorsed as helpful clarification and illustrative application of the articles of the confession. The accompanying unison readings for use in worship are samples of the ways in which this confession can be used widely in the church.

This confession guides the faith and life of the Mennonite Church and the General Conference Mennonite Church. Further, the *Confession of Faith in a Mennonite Perspective* is commended to all Christian churches and to those of other faiths or no faith, that they may seriously consider the claims of the gospel of Jesus Christ from this perspective. May these articles of faith encourage us to hold fast to the confession of our hope without wavering, for the One who has promised is faithful (Heb. 10:23). Praise and thanksgiving be to our God!

Article 1
God

We believe that God exists and is pleased with all who draw near by faith.[1] We worship the one holy and loving God who is Father, Son, and Holy Spirit eternally.[2] We believe that God has created all things visible and invisible, has brought salvation and new life to humanity through Jesus Christ, and continues to sustain the church and all things until the end of the age.

Beginning with Abraham and Sarah, God has called forth a people of faith to worship God alone, to witness to the divine purposes for human beings and all of creation, and to love their neighbors as themselves.[3] We have been joined to this people through the faithfulness of Jesus Christ and by confessing him to be Savior and Lord as the Holy Spirit has moved us.[4]

We humbly recognize that God far surpasses human comprehension and understanding.[5] We also gratefully acknowledge that God has spoken to humanity and related to us in many and various ways. We believe that God has spoken above all in the only Son, the Word who became flesh and revealed the divine being and character.[6]

God's awesome glory and enduring compassion are perfect in holy love. God's sovereign power and unending mercy are perfect in almighty love. God's knowledge of all things and care for creation are perfect in preserving love. God's abounding grace and wrath against sinfulness are perfect in righteous love. God's readiness to forgive and power to transform are perfect in redemptive love. God's unlimited justice and continuing patience with humankind are perfect in suffering love. God's infinite freedom and constant self-giving are perfect in faithful love.[7] To the one holy and ever-loving triune God be glory for ever and ever!

(1) Exod. 3:13-14; Heb. 11:6. (2) Exod. 20:1-6; Deut. 6:4; Matt. 28:19; 2 Cor. 13:13 [14]. (3) Gen. 12:2-3; Lev. 19:18; Rom. 4:11-25; 1 Pet. 3:9-11. (4) Gal. 2:20; Rom. 3:22. (5) Exod. 3:13-14; Job 37; Isa. 40:18-25; Rom. 11:33-36. (6) John 1:14, 18; Heb. 1:1-4. (7) Exod. 20:4-6; 34:5-7; Ps. 25:4-10; Isa. 6; 54:10; Matt. 5:48; Rom. 2:5-11; 3:21-26; 1 John 4:8, 16.

Commentary

1. We believe that what we know of God through revelation fits with who God really is. To confess that God is Father, Son, and Holy Spirit is to confess that the Son and the Holy Spirit are fully divine. It is also to confess that God is one and that God's oneness is the unity of Father, Son, and Holy Spirit (for example, John 10:30; 14:18-20; 16:12-15; 20:21-22). In this confession, the word *God* can refer to the God who is triune or to the first person of the trinity. (On *God* as the first person of the trinity, compare Matt. 28:19 with 2 Cor. 13:13[14] and numerous other passages.)

Confessing God as Father, Son, and Holy Spirit also emphasizes the shared work of creation, salvation, and the final consummation. This trinitarian understanding of God has implications for ethics. The ethical standards we receive from God as Creator are not contrary to those which are revealed by God as Redeemer. For example, we cannot claim that God as Creator justifies Christian participation in violence, while God as Redeemer calls us to make peace without violence. What the Creator intends for human conduct has been most fully revealed in Jesus Christ.

Some early Christian creeds express a trinitarian understanding of God with the terms *essence, substance,* or *person.* Early

Anabaptist writers such as Menno Simons and Pilgram Marpeck used mainly biblical language to refer to the triune God. They also used some concepts from the early creeds. Some Mennonite confessions of faith have used only biblical terminology to refer to God; others have used both biblical and creedal language. This confession assumes basic agreement with traditional confessions of faith, though it remains with biblical terminology for the most part. The article uses the word *triune*, which is not found in Scripture. Yet, it is an apt term for the God revealed in Scripture and helps maintain a biblically based theological and ethical balance.

2. The relation between God and the people of faith is the context within which we have received God's revelation and which provides the basis for our understanding of God. Our knowledge of God comes mainly from this relationship and its history, which began with God calling out the household of Abraham and Sarah. (See Heb. 11:8-12 and note the oldest texts for verse 11: "By faith Sarah . . . received power to conceive . . . because she considered him faithful who had promised.") At the same time, we believe that the God whom we confess is the one and only true God of all creation and of all humanity. Even before calling a particular people, God was revealed through creation and spoke to humanity.

3. God both surpasses human understanding and is truly knowable through revelation. Our knowledge of God rests in this tension. Further, God's characteristics (or "attributes") sometimes appear contradictory to us. For example, how can God be both just and merciful, characteristics which in human experience often seem opposed? Yet we confess that in the divine being these attributes are perfectly united. Finally, according to Scripture, the love of God has a certain priority in relation to other divine attributes. The article reflects this emphasis by such phrases as "righteous love" rather than by playing "righteousness" off against "love" or by focusing on one without the other.

Article 2
Jesus Christ

We believe in Jesus Christ, the Word of God become flesh. He is the Savior of the world, who has delivered us from the dominion of sin and reconciled us to God by humbling himself and becoming obedient unto death on a cross.[1] He was declared to be Son of God with power by his resurrection from the dead.[2] He is the head of the church, the exalted Lord, the Lamb who was slain, coming again to reign with God in glory. "No other foundation can anyone lay than that which is laid, which is Jesus Christ."[3]

We confess Jesus as the Christ, the Messiah, through whom God has prepared the new covenant for all peoples. Born of the seed of David, Jesus Christ fulfills the messianic promises given through Israel.[4] As prophet, he has proclaimed the coming of God's kingdom and called everyone to repent. As teacher of divine wisdom, he has made known God's will for human conduct. As faithful high priest, he has made the final atonement for sin and now intercedes for us. As king who chose the way of the cross, he has revealed the servant character of divine power.[5]

We accept Jesus Christ as the Savior of the world.[6] In his ministry of preaching, teaching, and healing, he proclaimed forgiveness of sins and peace to those near at hand and those far off.[7] In calling disciples to follow him, he began the new community of faith.[8] In his suffering, he loved his enemies and did not resist them with violence, thus giving us an example to follow.[9] In the shedding of his blood on the cross, Jesus offered up his life to the Father, bore the sins of all, and reconciled us to God.[10] God then raised him from the dead, thereby conquering death and disarming the powers of sin and evil.[11]

We acknowledge Jesus Christ as the only Son of God, the Word of God incarnate. He was conceived of the Holy Spirit and born of the Virgin Mary. As fully human and tempted as we are, yet without sin, he is the model human being.[12] As fully divine, he is the one in whom the fullness of God was pleased to dwell. During his earthly life, Jesus had an intimate relationship with his heavenly Abba and taught his disciples to pray "Abba, Father."[13] He is the image of the invisible God, and "all things have been created through him and for him, for he is before all things."[14]

We recognize Jesus Christ as the head of the church, his body.[15] As members of his body, we are in Christ, and Christ dwells in us. Empowered by this intimate relationship with Christ, the church continues his ministry of mercy, justice, and peace in a broken world.[16]

We worship Jesus Christ as the one whom God has exalted and made Lord over all. He is our Lord and the not-yet-recognized Lord of the world. We live in the assurance of his coming again as the one by whom all humanity will be judged. He is the one who shall be acknowledged Lord of all, and the Lamb who will reign forever and ever.[17]

(1) Phil. 2:5-8. (2) Rom. 1:4. (3) 1 Cor. 3:11. (4) 2 Sam. 7:13-14; Isa. 9:1-6; Rom. 1:3; 2 Cor. 6:18. (5) Isa. 42:1-9; Matt. 4:17; Luke 4:43f.; Matt. 5–7; Heb. 2:17; 1 Pet. 3:18; Rom. 8:34; Heb. 7:25; John 18:36-37; Rev. 5:8-14; 7:17. (6) Acts 4:12; 1 John 4:14. (7) Eph. 2:13-22. (8) Mark 3:13-19. (9) Matt. 26:50; 1 Pet. 2:21-23. (10) Luke 23:46; Rom. 5:18; 2 Cor. 5:19. (11) Col. 2:15; Eph. 1:20-21. (12) Heb. 4:15; Rom. 5:14-21; 1 Pet. 2:21. (13) Mark 14:36; Matt. 6:9-13; Rom. 8:15; Gal. 4:6. (14) Col. 1:15-17,

19. (15) Eph. 1:22-23. (16) Col. 1:24. (17) Acts 17:31; Phil. 2:11; Rev. 5:12-14.

Commentary

1. This article reflects biblical understandings of Jesus Christ in an Anabaptist-Mennonite perspective. It stresses, for example, Jesus' obedience and suffering in his work of atonement, his humility and servanthood as the pathway to exaltation, the believers' experience of Christ in the community of faith, the integration of faith and ethics, and peace as central to the character of Christ. These themes belong to the heart of the gospel.

2. In some Protestant traditions, the Messiah (the Anointed One) is identified as prophet, priest, and king—the offices for which people were anointed in Old Testament times (Isa. 61:1; Exod. 29:29; 1 Sam. 10:10). This confession also identifies Jesus as teacher, against the backdrop of Old Testament wisdom literature (for example, some of the Psalms, Proverbs, Job, and Ecclesiastes). As disciples, we participate in this fourfold work of Christ.

3. For centuries, Christian creeds have confessed that Jesus Christ has both a human and a divine nature. The Bible does not use the language of "natures" to describe Jesus Christ. When using this language, we should not overemphasize either the human or the divine side. This way of speaking about Jesus Christ can be helpful if it upholds what the Bible reveals to us about him.

4. As Son of God, Jesus Christ shares fully in the character and work of the triune God (Matt. 11:27; John 1:1-3; 7–8; Col. 1:15-20; Eph. 1:3-14). For example, the Bible teaches that Christ participated in creation; he was one with God from the beginning (Col. 1:16). His intimate unity with the Holy Spirit through his Father is revealed in Jesus' words of comfort to the disciples: Jesus said that the Father will send the Advocate, the Holy Spirit, in Jesus' name, who will teach the disciples and remind them of

what Jesus told them (John 14:26). While on earth, Jesus addressed God with the Aramaic term of endearment "Abba," used in his day to express an intimate father-child relationship, much as we might say "Daddy."

Article 3
Holy Spirit

We believe in the Holy Spirit, the eternal Spirit of God, who dwelled in Jesus Christ, who empowers the church, who is the source of our life in Christ, and who is poured out on those who believe as the guarantee of our redemption and of the redemption of creation.

Through the Spirit of God, the world was created, prophets and writers of Scripture were inspired, the people were enabled to follow God's law, Mary conceived, and Jesus was anointed at his baptism.[1] By the power of the Holy Spirit, Jesus proclaimed the good news of the reign of God, healed the sick, accepted death on the cross, and was raised from the dead.

At Pentecost, God began to pour out the Spirit on all flesh and to gather the church from among many nations.[2] As a dwelling place of the Holy Spirit, the church praises and worships God and brings forth the fruit of the Spirit. By the gifts of the Holy Spirit, all Christians are called to carry out their particular ministries. By the guidance of the Holy Spirit, the church comes to unity in doctrine and action. By the power of the Holy Spirit, the church preaches, teaches, testifies, heals, loves, and suffers, following the example of Jesus its Lord.

The Holy Spirit calls people to repentance, convicts them of sin, and leads into the way of righteousness all those who open themselves to the working of the Spirit.[3] Scripture urges us to yield to the Spirit, and not to resist or quench the Spirit.[4] By water and the Spirit, we are born anew into the family of God. The Spirit dwells in each child of God, bringing us into relationship with God. Through the indwelling of the Spirit, we are made heirs together with Christ, if we suffer with him, so that we may also be glorified with him.[5] The Spirit teaches us, reminds us of Jesus' word, guides us into all truth, and empowers us to speak the word of God with boldness.[6]

The Holy Spirit enables our life in Christian community, comforts us in suffering, is present with us in time of persecution, intercedes for us in our weakness, guarantees the redemption of our bodies, and assures the future redemption of creation.[7]

(1) Ps. 104:30; Mic. 3:8; Ezek. 36:26-27; Luke 1:35; 3:22. (2) Joel 2:28-29; Acts 2:16-18. (3) John 16:8-10. (4) Isa. 63:10; Acts 5:3; Eph. 4:30; 1 Thess. 5:19. (5) John 3:5; Rom. 8:14-17. (6) John 14:26; 16:13; 1 Cor. 2:14; Acts 4:24-31. (7) Matt. 10:20; 2 Cor. 5:5; Rom. 8:26-27; Eph. 1:13-14; Rom. 8:18-23.

Commentary

1. According to Scripture, the Spirit of God is God's presence and power active in the world. The Spirit, or breath, of God acted in creation (Gen. 1:2) and continues to act in the creative process throughout the world, in expected and unexpected places. God's Spirit was a source of power and revealed God's wisdom to prophets and other holy people. By the power of the Spirit, Jesus healed the sick, cast out unclean spirits, and proclaimed the reign of God (Matt. 12:28; Luke 3:22; 5:17). By the same Spirit, he offered his life to God (Heb. 9:14) and was raised from the dead (Rom. 8:11). This Spirit of God and Spirit of Jesus is the Holy Spirit, who is one with the Father and the Son.

2. The Gospel of John (1–16) and the letters of Paul use similar language to describe the work of the Spirit of God and

the Spirit of Christ—or the Spirit and Christ. Even though each has a particular role, the work of the Holy Spirit since Christ's exaltation always conforms to Jesus Christ. So, Christ is the standard for discerning which spirit is of God (1 Cor. 12:3; John 14:26; 1 John 4:2-3). Only that Spirit which conforms to Jesus Christ, as we know him through the Scriptures, can reliably guide our faith and life.

3. The New Testament affirms that, since the resurrection, we are living in a new period of God's action in the world, the age of the Spirit. No longer is the Spirit present only with a few; now the Spirit is poured out on "all flesh," that is, on male and female, young and old, slave and free (Acts 2:16-21), people of all ethnic backgrounds who are being gathered into the people of God (Acts 10–11). By the Holy Spirit, the love of God is poured into our hearts (Rom. 5:5). We are adopted as children of God (Gal. 4:6-7) and experience new birth into the family of God. This presence of the Holy Spirit is connected with being "in Christ," being part of the body of Christ.

4. The anointing of the Holy Spirit is offered to all people. But those who do evil do not come to the light for fear that their deeds may be exposed (John 3:17-21). Those who have repented of sin (Acts 2:38) and are coming to the light are the ones who receive the Spirit. We are most open to the Spirit's work in us when we are becoming poor in spirit—emptying ourselves of all that is foreign to the way of the cross and committing ourselves to a life of love and the service of God. At the same time, the Holy Spirit gives us power to proclaim the word with boldness, to love enemies, to suffer in hope, to remain faithful in trials, and to rejoice in everything. As we walk by the Spirit, the Spirit produces the fruit of love, joy, peace, patience, kindness, goodness, faithfulness, gentleness, and self-control (Gal. 5:22-23).

5. Both the church and the individual Christian are the temple of the Holy Spirit (Eph. 2:22; 1 Cor. 6:19). The Spirit of

Christ is in the midst of the church in its gathering for prayer and praise. By the gifts of the Spirit, given to each member, the church builds itself up in love (Eph. 4:1-16; 1 Cor. 12–13) and is given the unity of the Holy Spirit (2 Cor. 13:13). By the guidance of the Holy Spirit, the church makes decisions, disciplines, and encourages its members.

6. Prophecy is one of the gifts given to the church by the Holy Spirit (1 Cor. 12:28; Rom. 12:6; Eph. 4:11). Yet, some Christians have asserted that prophecy and revelation stopped after the time of the apostles. They say that the main way in which the Holy Spirit continues to reveal truth is through helping us to interpret Scripture. Others have claimed that present revelations are on an equal basis with Scripture or even have priority over it.

We know from Scripture that the Holy Spirit continues to reveal God's will to us (1 Cor. 14:26-33). The Spirit of God is not silent in the present. However, this new revelation will not contradict what we know of Christ's way in Scripture (John 14:26). So we can open ourselves to revelation and prophecy, provided we test them in the community of faith by the norm provided in Christ through the Scriptures.

Article 4
Scripture

We believe that all Scripture is inspired by God through the Holy Spirit for instruction in salvation and training in righteousness. We accept the Scriptures as the Word of God and as the fully reliable and trustworthy standard for Christian faith and life. We seek to understand and interpret Scripture in harmony with Jesus Christ as we are led by the Holy Spirit in the church.

We believe that God was at work through the centuries in the process by which the books of the Old and New Testaments were inspired and written.[1] Through the Holy Spirit, God moved human witnesses to write what is needed for salvation, for guidance in faith and life, and for devotion to God.[2]

We accept the Bible as the Word of God written. God has spoken in many and various ways through the prophets and apostles.[3] God has spoken above all in the living Word who became flesh and revealed the truth of God faithfully and without deception.[4] We also acknowledge the Scripture as the fully reliable and trustworthy Word of God written in human language.[5] We believe that God continues to speak through the living and written Word.[6] Because Jesus Christ is the Word become flesh, Scripture as a whole has its center and fulfillment in him.[7]

We acknowledge the Scripture as the authoritative source and standard for preaching and teaching about faith and life, for distinguishing truth from error, for discerning between good and evil, and for guiding prayer and worship. Other claims on our understanding of Christian faith and life, such as tradition, culture, experience, reason, and political powers, need to be tested and corrected by the light of Holy Scripture.[8]

The Bible is the essential book of the church. Through the Bible, the Holy Spirit nurtures the obedience of faith to Jesus Christ and guides the church in shaping its teaching, witnessing, and worship. We commit ourselves to persist and delight in reading, studying, and meditating on the Scriptures.[9] We participate in the church's task of interpreting the Bible and of discerning what God is saying in our time by examining all things in the light of Scripture.[10] Insights and understandings which we bring to the interpretation of the Scripture are to be tested in the faith community.

(1) Jer. 30:2; Jer. 36; 2 Tim. 3:16. (2) 2 Pet. 1:21. (3) Exod. 20:1; Jer. 1:9-10; Gal. 1:11-12; Heb. 1:1-4. (4) John 1:14, 18; Rev. 19:13. (5) Prov. 30:5; John 10:35. (6) Isa. 55:10-11; John 20:31. (7) Matt. 5:17; Luke 24:27; Acts 4:11. (8) Mark 7:13; Acts 5:29-32; Col. 2:6-23. (9) Ps. 1:2; 1 Tim. 4:13; 2 Tim. 3:15-17. (10) Acts 15:13-20; Heb. 4:2-8, 12.

Commentary

1. According to Scripture, the term "the Word of the Lord" or "the Word of God" or "the Word" refers to:

—a message that God has communicated through persons in the Old and New Testaments, especially through Moses, the prophets, and the apostles (for example, Exod. 20:1; Jer. 1:9-10; Acts 13:44-47);

—Jesus' proclamation of the kingdom of God (for example, Luke 4:43–5:1);

—the preached gospel of Jesus Christ (for example, Acts 8:25; 18:5; Col. 1:25-27; 1 Thess. 2:13);

—the living Word of God who became flesh in Jesus Christ (John 1:1, 14);

—a word or words from God that have been put into writing (for example, Jer. 36:4; John 15:25; Heb. 4:1-12).

Referring to the Bible as the Word of God therefore means, first of all, emphasizing the richness and scope of "the Word" in the Bible. Limiting the term "the Word of God" to its written form blinds us to the total witness of Scripture. Second, in referring to the Bible as the Word of God written, we are acknowledging its authority for the church. All other claims to represent an authoritative word on matters of faith and life must be measured and corrected by Scripture through the guidance of the Holy Spirit in the community of faith.

2. The authority of Scripture has its ultimate source in God, who has inspired ("breathed") it for specific purposes in the life of the church and its members (2 Tim. 3:16-17). The church confesses and recognizes the authority of Holy Scripture; it does not take upon itself the right to give the Scripture its authority. Precisely how God has inspired the Scriptures through the Holy Spirit is not explained in the Bible. We therefore content ourselves with the assurance that Scripture is fully reliable and trustworthy because the One who has inspired it is faithful and true.

3. We recognize the 39 books of the Old Testament and the 27 books of New Testament as belonging to inspired Scripture. What we call the Old Testament was accepted by Israel as the standard for faith and life in three stages over several centuries: the law, the prophets, and the writings. The Old Testament, the Gospels, the Pauline letters, and gradually the rest of the New Testament were broadly recognized by the church as Holy Scripture by the fourth century.

4. Since the beginning of the Anabaptist reformation in sixteenth-century Europe, Mennonites have sought to be a biblical people in ways that both borrowed from the Protestant reformation and differed from it. Mennonites have shared the traditional Protestant emphasis on the authority of Scripture for

doctrine. In addition, Mennonites have underscored the following emphases:

—the authority of Scripture for ethics, for the relation of the church to society, and for church polity.

—the interpretation of Scripture in harmony with Jesus Christ, in the sense that his life, teachings, death, and resurrection are essential to understanding the Bible as a whole.

—the congregation of believers as the place where individual understandings and interpretations of Scripture are to be tested.

This confessional statement assumes and affirms these emphases.

Article 5
Creation and Divine Providence

We believe that God has created the heavens and the earth and all that is in them,[1] and that God preserves and renews what has been made. All creation ultimately has its source outside itself and belongs to the Creator. The world has been created good because God is good and provides all that is needed for life.[2]

We believe that the universe has been called into being as an expression of God's love and sovereign freedom alone. Creation witnesses to the eternal power and divine nature of God, who gives meaning and purpose to life and who alone is worthy of worship and praise.[3]

We acknowledge that God sustains creation in both continuity and change. We believe that God upholds order in creation and limits the forces of sin and evil for the sake of preserving and renewing humanity and the world.[4] God also works to save human beings and the world from death and destruction and to overcome the forces of sin and evil.

We therefore are called to respect the natural order of creation and to entrust ourselves to God's care and keeping, whether in adversity or plenty. Neither the work of human hands, nor the forces of the natural world around us, nor the power of the nations among which we live are worthy of the trust and honor due the Creator on whom they depend.[5]

(1) Gen. 1:1; Isa. 45:11f.; John 1:3. (2) Gen. 1:31; 1 Tim. 4:4. (3) Ps. 19:1-6; Rom. 1:19-23. (4) Gen. 9:8-17; Ps. 104; Eph. 3:9-11. (5) Ps. 33; Matt. 6:25-33; Matt. 10:26-31.

Commentary

1. In confessing God as Creator, we refer to the one and tri-une God, who is Father, Son, and Holy Spirit, according to the Scriptures. Creation should be understood as the work of the tri-une God, not as the work of the Father or Son or the Holy Spirit alone (Heb. 1:2-3; Col. 1:16; 1 Cor. 8:5-6; John 1:3, 14-18).

Some ways of speaking about God may undermine the full confession of the triune God as Creator. For example, speaking of God only as "Creator, Redeemer, and Sustainer" rather than as "Father, Son, and Holy Spirit" may promote the mistaken understanding that the "Father" alone is "Creator," the "Son" alone is "Redeemer," and the "Holy Spirit" alone is "Sustainer."

2. We speak of creation as an "expression" of God because of biblical references to creation by the divine word (Gen. 1; Ps. 148:5; John 1:1f.; Rom. 4:17). In many creation stories of other religions in Bible times, the world comes into being as an extension of the god or gods. In these accounts, the world shares in divinity, or is itself divine. In contrast, the biblical account of creation by the word of God clearly distinguishes between God the Creator and what has been created. The biblical refusal to confuse the created with the Creator, or to ascribe divinity to the world, fits with the Bible's rejection of idolatry in all its forms (Isa. 45:12-21; Acts 17:22-29).

When we confess that God is the Creator of the universe, we reject the idea that the world came into being without God. Nor do we accept the view that God made the world out of something which had existed before the time of creation or the view that matter is co-eternal with God. Scripture is clear that God was before anything else existed. Thus, both the Old Testament word for *create* and the witness of Scripture as a whole imply what theology has called "creation out of nothing."

As Creator, God is ultimately owner of the earth. God has given the earth to human beings to care for as God's stewards. See "The Creation and Calling of Human Beings" (Article 6) and "Christian Stewardship" (Article 21).

3. God continues to sustain and care for the world rather than leaving it to itself. Although sin and evil have damaged God's original creation, God continues to use the natural order, family, culture, and social and political systems to sustain life and to limit the forces of evil (Gen. 4:15; Ps. 34; Isa. 19:12-25; Matt. 6:25-30; John 5:17; Col. 1:15-17). Even though natural disasters cause havoc in the world, God continues to preserve creation and humanity from total destruction (Gen. 8:21-22). Therefore we need not be overcome by the fear of natural forces and other human beings which may cause suffering, persecution, or even death.

We are called to entrust ourselves to God's care, rather than finding our security in technology, in the elements of the natural world, or in the nations in which we live. We accept and use the resources of nature, society, and technology, so far as they sustain and enhance the quality of human life and the world around us in harmony with God's purposes, and so far as they do not undermine trust in God's providential care.

4. God not only preserves the world, but also acts to save the chosen people from evil and to bless all peoples and the rest of creation. God used elements of nature to free the Hebrew people from slavery in Egypt, to provide them with food, to accompany the revealing of the Law at Sinai, and to provide them with a dwelling place (Exod. 6–16; 19; Ps. 124; 136).

Because God works in ever new and surprising ways, creation is open to change. God also works to bring newness into creation for the sake of the covenant people and for all nations (Isa. 42:5-9; 44:21-28). See "Salvation" (Article 8) and "The Reign of God" (Article 24) on the renewal of creation in Jesus Christ and, through the work of the Holy Spirit, in the church and the world.

Article 6

The Creation and Calling of Human Beings

We believe that God has created human beings in the divine image. God formed them from the dust of the earth and gave them a special dignity among all the works of creation. Human beings have been made for relationship with God, to live in peace with each other, and to take care of the rest of creation.

We believe that human beings were created good, in the image of God.[1] As creatures according to the divine likeness, we have been made stewards to subdue and to care for creation out of reverence and honor for the Creator.[2] As creatures made in the divine image, we have been blessed with the abilities to respond faithfully to God, to live in harmony with other human beings, and to engage in meaningful work and rest. Because both Adam and Eve were equally and wonderfully made in the divine image, God's will from the beginning has been for women and men to live in loving and mutually helpful relationships with each other.[3]

We are grateful that God patiently preserves humanity and faithfully remains with us even through death.[4] God has made provision for the salvation of humanity and the redemption of creation.[5] We believe that the image of God in all its fullness has been revealed and restored in Jesus Christ, in whom we find our true humanity.[6]

(1) Gen. 1:26-27, 31; Rom. 8:29. (2) Gen. 1:26-30; Ps. 8:5-8; Rom. 1:21-23. (3) Gen. 2:18-23; Eph. 5:21-33. (4) Rom. 8:38-39. (5) Rom. 8:19-25. (6) 2 Cor. 4:4; Col. 1:15.

Commentary

1. The "image of God" refers to the unique relationship of human beings to God and therefore also to their distinctive relationship to each other and to the rest of creation. The term refers to human beings as a whole rather than to one particular aspect of the person.

Some theological understandings of human beings have focused on humanity's role as God's representative on earth to manage and care for it. Some have emphasized the relationship between men and women as a symbol of the inner relationships of the triune God. Other views have underscored the distinctive relationship with God for which human beings have been created. And some have focused on the differences between human beings and animals, especially human reason, culture, and morality. Each of these views emphasizes one aspect of the larger biblical picture of being human, which this article has summarized as being in the image and likeness of God.

2. According to Genesis 1:26-27, God created both man and woman in the divine image. Both are equal in relation to God and are created for relationship with each other. Woman's relation to God is not derived from man, and man's relation to God is not derived from woman. Genesis 2:18 describes woman as man's "helper," but this does not imply one-sided subordination. The same Hebrew word is most often used for God as "help" or "helper" (for example, in Deut. 33:7, 26; Ps. 33:20; 54:4; 70:5; 115:9-11). The rule of man over woman is a result of sin (Gen. 3:16) and is therefore not an acceptable order among the redeemed (Gal. 3:28; 1 Cor. 7:4; 11:11-12).

The renewal of humanity in Jesus Christ restores both woman and man to the divine image. On Pentecost, the Holy Spirit was poured out upon both men and women directly in accord with the prophecy of Joel (Acts 2:1-18; see also Acts 1:12-

14). In the community of faith, Gentiles have the same status as Jews, slaves as free, and women as men (2 Cor. 6:18). They are called to live in unity with each other (Gal. 3:25-28) and in mutual subjection to each other (Eph. 5:21–6:9).

3. We believe that God created human beings with an ability to choose to obey or to disobey the word of God (Gen. 2:15-17). Humanity has been created with the freedom to choose the bond of a covenant relationship with God or to choose bondage to sin (Rom. 6:16-18). We are genuinely free only when we live in covenant with God and in conformity to God's will.

4. We believe that God intends human work to be a way of caring for and ordering rather than exploiting the world which has been created. Work is necessary to sustain and enhance human life. It can also be a way to serve and witness to others in the spirit of Jesus Christ (Gen. 1:28; 2:15, 19-20; 2 Thess. 3:6-13; Eph. 4:28; 6:5-9). According to God's design, we are to balance work and rest, for our own good and for the good of the rest of creation. Above all, regular rest from work is intended to remind us of God's presence and of God's creating, liberating, healing, and saving activity (Exod. 20:8-11; Deut. 5:12-15; Mark 3:1-5; Heb. 4:9-11).

Because we are called to serve God in all of life, we also seek to follow Jesus Christ in the work we choose and in the way we carry out our work. See the articles on "Discipleship and the Christian Life" (Article 17), "Christian Stewardship" (Article 21), and "The Reign of God" (Article 24).

Article 7
Sin

We confess that, beginning with Adam and Eve, humanity has disobeyed God, given way to the tempter, and chosen to sin. Because of sin, all have fallen short of the Creator's intent, marred the image of God in which they were created, disrupted order in the world, and limited their love for others. Because of sin, humanity has been given over to the enslaving powers of evil and death.[1]

Sin is turning away from God and making gods of creation and of ourselves. We sin by making individual and group choices to do unrighteousness and injustice.[2] We sin by omitting to do good and neglecting to give God the glory due our Creator and Redeemer. In sinning, we become unfaithful to the covenant with God and with God's people, destroy right relationships, use power selfishly, do violence, and become separated from God. As a result, we are not able to worship God rightly.[3]

Through sin, the powers of domination, division, destruction, and death have been unleashed in humanity and in all of creation. They have, in turn, further subjected human beings to the power of sin and evil, and have increased burdensome work and barren rest. The more we sin, the more we become trapped in sin. By our sin we open ourselves to the bondage of demonic powers.[4] Because of sin and its consequences, the efforts of human beings on their own to do the good and to know the truth are constantly corrupted.[5]

The enslaving nature of sin is apparent in the powers of evil, which work through both individuals and groups and in the entire created order. These powers, principalities, and elemental spirits of the universe often hold people captive and work through political, economic, social, and even religious systems to turn people away from justice and righteousness.[6] But thanks be to God, who has not allowed the powers to reign supreme over creation or left humanity without hope.

(1) Gen. 2:17; 3:22-24; 6:11-12; Rom. 1:21-32; 6:23.
(2) Dan. 9. (3) Isa. 1:12-17. (4) Rom. 6:12-18; Eph. 6:10-12. (5) Ps. 14:2-4; Rom. 3:9-18. (6) Eph. 2:1-3; Gal. 4:1-3.

Commentary

1. Sin is a reality, not an illusion. We cannot explain away sin by blaming it on illness or by claiming we are victims of circumstances or of evil. Sin involves personal responsibility and has real consequences. In Scripture, responsibility for sin and evil is ascribed not only to men and women. It is also ascribed to a personal power who is given various names: "serpent" (Gen. 3:1; 2 Cor. 11:3), "tempter" (Matt. 4:3), "Satan" (Zech. 3:1), "father of lies" (John 8:44), the "evil one" (Matt. 6:13), and "the devil" (James 4:7).

2. In addition, "powers," "principalities," "gods of the nations," and "elemental spirits of the universe," though not necessarily evil, are prone to distort God's purposes for them. They can corrupt and enslave humanity (Isa. 42:17; 45:20; Gal. 4:9; Eph. 2:1-3; 6:12; Col. 2:15). Sin is thus not only an individual matter, but involves groups, nations, and structures. Such organizations have a "spirit" that can incite persons to do evil they would not have chosen on their own. Governments, military forces, economic systems, educational or religious institutions, family systems, and structures determined by class, race, gender, or nationality are susceptible to demonic spirits. Human violence toward each other, enmity between peoples, the domination of men over women, and the adverse conditions of life and

work in the world—these are all signs of sin in humanity and in all creation (Gen. 3:14-19; 4:3-16; 6:11-13; 11:1-9; Rom. 8:21).

3. People sin not only by breaking particular divine laws, but also by breaking the covenant God offers to all. A covenant is an agreement that establishes a relationship. In the Bible, God initiates the covenant with God's people (Josh. 24:16-18; Jer. 7:23; 31:31-34; Hos. 2:18-23). *Faith* or *faithfulness* (English words used to translate the same word in the biblical languages) means living rightly within the covenant relationship. Thus, sin is fundamentally unfaithfulness to our relationship with God and disobedience to God's will. *Unrighteousness* and *injustice* include all sin; the same word in the biblical languages can be translated with either English word. Hebrew and Greek do not divide (as English does) between the individual dimension of sin (unrighteousness) and sin's social dimension (injustice).

4. Sin is part of the human condition; we all participate in it. The sin of Adam and Eve affects all (Rom. 5:12, 19); at the same time, we are held accountable for our own behavior. As the Anabaptist leader Pilgram Marpeck wrote, any heritage we have received from our first parents does not deprive us of our own final responsibility before God (Ezek. 18). Although human beings have free will, choice is limited. By the grace of God, we have been given the freedom to choose the bond of covenant relationship with God or to choose bondage to sin (Rom. 6:16-18), which leads to final separation from God. The Scriptures issue stern warnings that those who do not fear God, but persist in anger, lust, power mongering, and the like, face the destruction of hell (Matt. 5:22, 29; 18:9). See "The Reign of God" (Article 24).

5. Human sinfulness affects the entire person. No one aspect of human beings, such as reason or sexuality or the physical body, should be singled out as the primary carrier of sinfulness. Giving way to the "flesh" is expressed in a variety of sinful attitudes and behaviors (Rom. 13:14; Gal. 5:16, 24; 1 Cor. 11:18-30; Phil. 3:3-7).

6. Just as sin has marred the relations between human beings, so the effects of sin and evil have distorted human work and rest. Work has not been cursed by God (Ps. 104:23-24), but neither should it be idealized. According to Genesis 3:17, God did not curse work directly, but the "ground," that is, the conditions under which work is carried out in a world affected by sin and evil.

Article 8
Salvation

We believe that, through the life, death, and resurrection of Jesus Christ, God offers salvation from sin and a new way of life to all people. We receive God's salvation when we repent of sin and accept Jesus Christ as Savior and Lord. In Christ, we are reconciled with God and brought into the reconciling community of God's people. We place our faith in God that, by the same power that raised Christ from the dead, we may be saved from sin to follow Christ in this life and to know the fullness of salvation in the age to come.

From the beginning, God has acted with grace and mercy to bring about salvation—through signs and wonders, by delivering God's people, and by making a covenant with Israel.[1] God so loved the world that, in the fullness of time, God sent his Son, whose faithfulness unto death on the cross has provided the way of salvation for all people.[2] By his blood shed for us, Christ inaugurated the new covenant.[3] He heals us, forgives our sins, and delivers us from the bondage of evil and from those who do evil against us.[4] By his death and resurrection, he breaks the powers of sin and death,[5] cancels our debt of sin,[6] and opens the way to new life.[7] We are saved by God's grace, not by our own merits.[8]

When we hear the good news of the love of God, the Holy Spirit moves us to accept the gift of salvation. God brings us into right relationship without coercion. Our response includes yielding to God's grace, placing full trust in God alone, repenting of sin, turning from evil, joining the fellowship of the redeemed, and showing forth the obedience of faith in word and deed.[9] When we who once were God's enemies are reconciled with God through Christ, we also experience reconciliation with others, especially within the church.[10] In baptism we publicly testify to our salvation and pledge allegiance to the one true God and to the people of God, the church. As we experience grace and the new birth, we are adopted into the family of God and become more and more transformed into the image of Christ.[11] We thus respond in faith to Christ and seek to walk faithfully in the way of Christ.

We believe that the salvation we already experience is but a foretaste of the salvation yet to come, when Christ will vanquish sin and death, and the redeemed will live in eternal communion with God.

(1) Ps. 74:12; Deut. 6:20-25; Exod. 20:1-17. (2) John 3:16; Gal. 4:4; Heb. 1:1-2. (3) Matt. 26:28; 1 Cor. 11:25. (4) Rom. 5:1-5; Mark 2:1-12. (5) Rom. 8:2; Heb. 2:14-15. (6) Rom. 3:24-25; Col. 2:13-14; Mark 10:45. (7) Rom. 6:4. (8) Eph. 2:8-9. (9) Rom. 1:5; Luke 19:8-10. (10) Rom. 5:6-10. (11) Rom. 12:2; 2 Cor. 3:18.

Commentary

1. In the history of Christian thought, there have been three major views of the atonement. Each has a basis in Scripture and contributes to our understanding of salvation. By breaking the power of sin and death, Christ is conqueror over evil (the Christ-the-victor view). By canceling our debt of sin, Christ is a sacrifice and pays the ransom on our behalf (substitutionary atonement). By opening the way to new life, Christ shows God's love, inspiring us to receive that love and love God and others in return (the moral-influence view).

2. People undergo a variety of experiences in accepting salvation. Some have crisis conversions, while others hear the proclamation of salvation and are gradually nurtured by the community of faith before they make a commitment. In either case, acceptance of salvation is a personal, voluntary decision. Salvation is not acquired automatically because we are born into a Christian family or grow up in the church.

3. This confession uses a variety of expressions for salvation. For example, salvation is often expressed as "justification by faith." The justification that is "reckoned" to us as salvation (Rom. 4:1-12) is experienced as a covenant relationship with God. A covenant is a binding agreement between two parties. God offers the relationship. The just, or righteous, person has received the offer, lives according to the covenant, and trusts in God's faithfulness. Justification by faith and faithful obedience to the covenant relationship are inseparable (Heb. 11). See "Discipleship and the Christian Life" (Article 17).

"New birth" is another way to express salvation. Human beings were created in the image of God. That is, they were children of God. When they sinned, they became children of the devil and lost their place in God's family (1 John 2:29–3:10). Through salvation, we are "born again" or adopted into the family of God (Gal. 3:23–4:7).

The New Testament frequently connects our salvation with peace (John 16:33; Rom. 5:1; 10:15). In doing so, it builds on the Old Testament concept of shalom. Through Christ's death on the cross, we have both peace with God and reconciliation within the church between groups which had been enemies (Eph. 2:14-17). Christ's suffering without taking revenge gives us an example; we can follow in his steps and live for righteousness (1 Pet. 2:19-24; Luke 6:35-36; Mark 8:34). See also "Peace, Justice, and Nonresistance" (Article 22).

4. God saves us as individuals in community. The Lord's saving activity embraced an entire people in bondage (Exod. 15). Jesus called a company of disciples. The church is the con-

text of the message of salvation (Eph. 2:11-22; 1 Pet. 2:1-10). There, covenants are made in the presence of witnesses, and members are held accountable. God's covenant with us also brings about right relationship within the people of God, in which former hostilities are reconciled.

5. According to the Bible, salvation includes not only forgiveness of sins which we have committed, but also rescue from powers of evil in which we have become entrapped (1 Pet. 2:24; Matt. 26:28; Heb. 2:14-15), deliverance from enemies who have sinned against us (Luke 21:16-19; Acts 4), and healing. For a discussion of the relationship of salvation and healing, see "The Church in Mission" (Article 10), Commentary paragraph 3. Our ultimate salvation lies in the power of the resurrection.

Article 9
The Church of Jesus Christ

We believe that the church is the assembly of those who have accepted God's offer of salvation through faith in Jesus Christ. The church is the new community of disciples sent into the world to proclaim the reign of God and to provide a foretaste of the church's glorious hope. The church is the new society established and sustained by the Holy Spirit. The church, the body of Christ, is called to become ever more like Jesus Christ, its head, in its worship, ministry, witness, mutual love and care, and the ordering of its common life.[1]

We acknowledge the church as the society of believers from many nations, anointed for witness by the Holy Spirit.[2] Through the work of the Holy Spirit, divisions between nations, races, classes, and genders are being healed as persons from every human grouping are reconciled and united in the church.[3] In times of suffering as well as tranquillity, the church depends on the Spirit's presence and power, rather than on the power or benevolence of government, for its preservation and mission.

The church is the assembly of those who voluntarily commit themselves to follow Christ in life and to be accountable to one another and to God, while recognizing that the church is imperfect and thus in constant need of repentance. The church's identity as God's people of faith is sustained and renewed as members gather regularly for worship. Here the church celebrates God's boundless grace, reaffirms its loyalty to God above all else, and seeks to discern God's will.

The church is the household, or family, of God.[4] Commitment to one another is shown in loving one another as God loves, in sharing material and spiritual resources, in exercising mutual care and discipline, and in showing hospitality to all.[5] The church welcomes all people who join themselves to Christ to become part of the family of God.[6]

We believe that the church as the body of Christ is the visible manifestation of Jesus Christ. The church is called to live and minister as Christ lived and ministered in the world. As many members belong to one body, so all believers have been baptized in one Spirit into the one body of Christ. There are varieties of gifts and ministries in the church, all given for the common good. Believers are to love each other and to grow toward the likeness of Christ, who is the head of the church.

The church exists as a community of believers in the local congregation, as a community of congregations, and as the worldwide community of faith.

(1) Eph. 4:13, 15. (2) Acts 1:8; 2:1-11. (3) Acts 11:1-18; 1 Cor. 12:12-13; Gal. 3:26-28. (4) Mark 3:33-35; Eph. 2:19. (5) Deut. 10:19; Rom. 12:13; Heb. 13:2. (6) John 20:21; Matt. 28:18-20; Matt. 5–7.

Commentary

1. New Testament references to the church as God's people (1 Pet. 2:10) show that the early church depended on the Old Testament for much of its self-understanding (Exod. 7:6; 2 Sam. 7:24). As in Old Testament times, the New Testament people of God see themselves as a covenant community, relying on God's promise of steadfast love and sustaining mercy. They are "a chosen race, a holy nation, God's own people" (1 Pet. 2:9; see Exod. 19:6). The word *church* is most often a translation of the Hebrew

qahal or the Greek *ekklesia,* meaning "assembly." But the church is a new kind of assembly. Its identity is not rooted in a common biological heritage or tied to one geographical location. The church is made up of people from many nations and ethnic backgrounds. Thus the church is a new social and political reality, described in this article with terms like "society," "assembly," "household of God," and "community of disciples."

2. Mennonite emphasis on voluntary church membership, together with the modern focus on human potential, may tempt us to regard the church merely as a product of human effort. But the church is more than a human organization. The church depends on God for its very being and life (Eph. 3:20-21). Its foundation is Jesus Christ (1 Cor. 3:11). It relies constantly on the Holy Spirit.

3. One of the Anabaptists' favorite images for the church was the "body of Christ." Participation in church life is a participation in Christ. Following Christ in life, a response of faithfulness to the baptismal covenant and to communal loyalty, is a way of knowing Christ. Works of love and service are an extension of Christ's ministry in and through his body, the church. Joining in corporate worship regularly (Heb. 10:25) and sharing in the Lord's Supper are ways of participating in the life of Christ and encouraging each other.

4. The articles that follow give more detail concerning the church: its mission (Article 10); its practices of baptism, the Lord's Supper, and foot washing (Articles 11-13); discipline, ministry, and order and unity (Articles 14-16). Later articles (17-24) discuss the church in the world and the relation between the church and the reign of God.

Article 10
The Church in Mission

We believe that the church is called to proclaim and to be a sign of the kingdom of God. Christ has commissioned the church to be his witnesses, making disciples of all nations, baptizing them, and teaching them to observe all things he has commanded.[1]

In his mission of preaching, teaching, and healing, Jesus announced, "The kingdom of God has come near; repent, and believe in the good news."[2] After his death and resurrection, Jesus commissioned his disciples, saying, "Peace be with you. As the Father has sent me, so I send you. . . . Receive the Holy Spirit."[3] Empowered by that Spirit, we continue Jesus' ministry of gathering the new people of God, who acknowledge Christ as Lord and Savior.

The church is called to witness to the reign of Christ by embodying Jesus' way in its own life and patterning itself after the reign of God. Thus it shows the world a sample of life under the lordship of Christ. By its life, the church is to be a city on a hill, a light to the nations,[4] testifying to the power of the resurrection by a way of life different from the societies around it.

The church is also to give witness by proclaiming the reign of God in word and deed. The church is to seek the lost, call for repentance, announce salvation from sin, proclaim the gospel of peace, set free the oppressed, pray for righteousness and justice, serve as Jesus did, and without coercion urge all people to become part of the people of God. The church is called to be a channel of

God's healing, which may include anointing with oil.[5] Even at the risk of suffering and death, the love of Christ compels faithful witnesses to testify for their Savior.[6]

Such witness is a response to Jesus' call to make disciples. As they are welcomed and incorporated into the church, new Christians learn to participate in the church's worship, in its fellowship, education, mutual aid, decision making, service, and continuing mission.[7] New believers also help the church to learn new dimensions of its mission.[8]

God calls the church to direct its mission to people from all nations and ethnic backgrounds. Jesus commissioned his disciples to be his witnesses in "Jerusalem, in all Judea and Samaria, and to the ends of the earth."[9] The apostle Paul preached to the Gentile nations. The church today is also called to witness to people of every culture, ethnicity, or nationality. The mission of the church does not require the protection of any nation or empire. Christians are strangers and aliens within all cultures. Yet the church itself is God's nation, encompassing people who have come from every tribe and nation. Indeed, its mission is to reconcile differing groups, creating one new humanity[10] and providing a preview of that day when all the nations shall stream to the mountain of the Lord and be at peace.[11]

(1) Acts 1:8; Matt. 28:19-20. (2) Mark 1:15. (3) John 20:21-22; Acts 10:36. (4) Matt. 5:13-16; Isa. 42:6. (5) Mark 6:13; James 5:14-15. (6) 2 Cor. 5:14. (7) Acts 2:41-47. (8) Acts 10; 15. (9) Acts 1:8. (10) Eph. 2:15-16. (11) Isa. 2:2-4.

Commentary

1. Christ has commissioned the church to continue his mission. Missionaries and others with the gift of evangelism do not

function independently, but as representatives of Christ and the church. The commissions by Jesus to his disciples (recorded in Matt. 28:19-20; Mark 16:15-18; Luke 24:45-49; John 20:21-22; and Acts 1:8) are given through the apostles to the community as a whole.

2. The mission of the church involves both word and deed, evangelism and service, proclaiming Christ's message and demonstrating, by the life of the church, the nature of the new creation in Christ. Neither word alone nor deed alone is sufficient for mission. Word explains deed, and deed authenticates word.

3. In the ministry of Jesus, healing (in body and in spirit) and salvation are closely related. The same Greek word is used in the New Testament for *healing* and *salvation*. Jesus' words both to those whose sins were forgiven and to those who were healed were, "Your faith has saved you [made you well]; go in peace." (Compare Luke 7:50 and 8:48, where the same Greek words are used, but the NIV and NRSV use different English words.) The church continues Jesus' ministry of healing. The church may be a channel for healing through the service of prayer and anointing with oil.

4. Mission includes peace and evangelism. Peace is an integral part of the content of the church's message (Acts 10:36; Eph. 2:17; 6:15). Peace also describes the context of evangelism (John 20:21-22). The power of gospel is so strong and God's mercy is so wide that it is possible for any person to repent and be saved. No enemy is so evil as to be beyond God's love. The church lives and preaches reconciliation boldly, yet without coercion. The missionary church chooses to suffer rather than to force its way. In the language of the New Testament, the word for *witness* is the same as the word for *martyr*.

5. The church is called to live as an alternative culture within the surrounding society. Thus, the church is involved in cross-cultural mission whether it reaches out to people of the majority

culture, to people of minority cultures within the society, or to various cultural groups in other countries. The church lives within the dominant culture, yet is called to challenge that culture's myths and assumptions when they conflict with Christian faith. Those cultural myths include individualism, materialism, militarism, nationalism, racism, sexism, and a worldview which denies the reality of anything beyond the grasp of the five senses and reason.

6. In its mission, the church claims Jesus Christ as the only Savior of the world (Acts 4:12). Some people feel that all ways to God are equally valid and that mission work by its very nature is intolerant and coercive. However, faithful witness to Christ is noncoercive; it does not force our point of view on anyone. It recognizes that God is not left without a witness anywhere (Acts 10:35; 14:17; 17:22-31; Rom. 1:19-20; 2:14-16). It testifies to Christ's work in our lives and invites others to know him, follow him, and become part of his body. We engage in mission because of our love and concern for people and because the love of Christ urges us on. We understand also that mission helps us grow in our understanding of the gospel, just as the early church's mission to the Gentiles helped it understand the gospel in new ways.

Article 11
Baptism

We believe that the baptism of believers with water is a sign of their cleansing from sin. Baptism is also a pledge before the church of their covenant with God to walk in the way of Jesus Christ through the power of the Holy Spirit. Believers are baptized into Christ and his body by the Spirit, water, and blood.

Baptism is a testimony to God's gift of the Holy Spirit and the continuing work of the Spirit in the lives of believers. Through the Spirit we repent and turn toward God in faith. The baptism of the Holy Spirit enables believers to walk in newness of life, to live in community with Christ and the church, to offer Christ's healing and forgiveness to those in need, to witness boldly to the good news of Christ, and to hope in the sharing of Christ's future glory.

Baptism by water is a sign that a person has repented, received forgiveness, renounced evil, and died to sin,[1] through the grace of God in Christ Jesus. Thus cleansed, believers are incorporated into Christ's body on earth, the church. Baptism by water is also a pledge to serve Christ and to minister as a member of his body according to the gifts given to each one. Jesus himself requested water baptism at the beginning of his ministry and sent his followers to "make disciples of all nations, baptizing them in the name of the Father and of the Son and of the Holy Spirit."[2] Baptism is done in obedience to Jesus' command and as a public commitment to identify with Jesus Christ, not only in his baptism by water, but in his life in the Spirit and in his death in suffering love.

46

The baptism of blood, or baptism of suffering, is the offering of one's life, even to death. Jesus understood the giving of his life through the shedding of his blood for others as a baptism.[3] He also spoke about his disciples' suffering and death as a baptism.[4] Those who accept water baptism commit themselves to follow Jesus in giving their lives for others, in loving their enemies, and in renouncing violence, even when it means their own suffering or death.

Christian baptism is for those who confess their sins, repent, accept Jesus Christ as Savior and Lord, and commit themselves to follow Christ in obedience as members of his body, both giving and receiving care and counsel in the church. Baptism is for those who are of the age of accountability and who freely request baptism on the basis of their response to Jesus Christ in faith.[5]

(1) Rom. 6:1-4; Acts 2:38-39. (2) Matt. 28:19. (3) Luke 12:50; 1 John 5:7-8. (4) Mark 10:38. (5) Matt. 28:19-20; John 4:1; Acts 2:38; Gal. 3:27.

Commentary

1. Some churches refer to baptism and the Lord's Supper as symbols, sacraments, or ordinances. In this confession of faith, these ceremonies are called *signs*, a biblical term rich in meanings. Sign is, first of all, an act of God: signs and wonders in Egypt (Exod. 10:1; Num. 14:11), signs to prophets (Isa. 7:14; 55:13), and Jesus' performance of signs (John 2:11; 12:37; 20:30). John 2:18-22 sees Jesus' death and resurrection as a sign. A sign is not only an act of God, but a human action as well: eating unleavened bread at Passover (Exod. 13:9), binding of the commandments to oneself (Deut. 6:8), keeping of the Sabbath (Exod. 31:13; Ezek. 20:20). Likewise, baptism is a sign, representing both God's action in delivering us from sin and death and the action of the one who is baptized, who pledges to God to follow Jesus Christ within the context of Christ's body, the church.

2. First John 5:7-8 identifies three aspects of baptism: the Spirit and the water and the blood. This passage refers, first of all, to Jesus' baptism. But the New Testament also says that believers are to identify with Jesus.

The baptism of the Holy Spirit: According to the New Testament, water baptism and baptism with the Spirit are closely connected, though not always in the same way. The Holy Spirit rested on Jesus at the time of his baptism (John 1:33). In Acts, believers received the Holy Spirit before, with, or after water baptism.

The baptism of water: Baptism has its roots in the Old Testament practice of ceremonially washing what had become unclean through disease, sin, or other cause (Lev. 14:1-9; 16:24-30; 17:15-16). Gentiles were initiated into the covenant people with proselyte baptism. Christian water baptism signifies the cleansing of the person from sin and incorporation into the new community of faith. The church may baptize by pouring, immersion, or the sprinkling of water (Rom. 6:3-4; Col. 2:12; Acts 2:17; Tit. 3:5-7). Scripture also refers to baptism as a pledge to God (1 Pet. 3:21) and as a commitment to faithfulness and ministry (Rom. 6:1-11). Jesus' baptism can be seen in the light of this pledge. In the New Testament, baptism follows a person's faith. Baptism therefore is for those who are ready to enter a faithful relationship with Christ and the church.

Thus, baptism should always be done by the church and its representatives, if possible in the presence of the congregation. It should be public because baptism means a commitment to membership and service in a particular congregation. Thus, water baptism is to be reserved for those old enough to make such a pledge. Infants and children have no need for baptism, since they are safe in the care of God. When they are able to be accountable for their own actions, they are able to make the church's faith their own.

The baptism of blood: Baptism by water is also a pledge of the believer's acceptance of the baptism of suffering and death. Water baptism identifies us with Christ in his way of the cross and his resurrection (Rom. 6:5-11). We are buried with him "by baptism into death, so that as Christ was raised from the dead by

the glory of the Father, we too might walk in newness of life"
(Rom. 6:3-4).

Article 12
The Lord's Supper

We believe that the Lord's Supper is a sign by which the church thankfully remembers the new covenant which Jesus established by his death. In this communion meal, the members of the church renew our covenant with God and with each other. As one body, we participate in the life of Jesus Christ given for the redemption of humankind. Thus we proclaim the Lord's death until he comes.[1]

The Lord's Supper points to Jesus Christ, whose body was given for us and whose shed blood established the new covenant.[2] In sharing the bread and cup, each believer remembers the death of Jesus and God's act of deliverance in raising Jesus from the dead. As we relive this event with a common meal, we give thanks for all God's acts of deliverance in the past and present, for the forgiveness of sins, and for God's continuing grace in our lives.

The supper re-presents the presence of the risen Christ in the church. As we partake of the communion of the bread and cup, the gathered body of believers shares in the body and blood of Christ[3] and recognizes again that its life is sustained by Christ, the bread of life.

Remembering how Jesus laid down his life for his friends, we his followers recommit ourselves to the way of the cross. Confessing our sins to one another and receiving forgiveness, we are to come as one body to the table of the Lord. There we renew our baptismal covenant with God and with each other and recognize our unity with all believers everywhere in all times.

All are invited to the Lord's table who have been baptized into the community of faith, are living at peace with God and with their brothers and sisters in the faith, and are willing to be accountable in their congregation.

Celebrating the Lord's Supper in this manner, the church looks forward in joy and hope to the feast of the redeemed with Christ in the age to come.[4]

(1) 1 Cor. 11:26. (2) Jer. 31:31-34; 1 Cor. 11:24-25.
(3) 1 Cor. 10:16. (4) Luke 22:15-20, 28-30.

Commentary

1. On the night that he was betrayed, Jesus and his disciples gathered to eat the Passover meal. This annual celebration called to remembrance God's great act of delivering the people of Israel from slavery in Egypt (Exod. 12). Jesus' Last Supper signaled that he was leading his followers in a new exodus out of bondage and into salvation. Through Jesus' death and resurrection, God has rescued believers from sin and evil and brought them into a new covenant. The new people of God created through this covenant is continuous with the people of the old covenant, whom God rescued from bondage in Egypt. The people of the new covenant includes all who have confessed Jesus Christ as Lord and Savior.

2. The bread of the Lord's Supper is a sign of Christ's body, and the cup is a sign of the new covenant in his blood (Luke 22:19-20). As Christians eat the bread and drink the cup, they experience Christ's presence in their midst. The Lord's Supper both represents Christ and is a way in which Christ is present again ("re-present") in the body of believers. In this meal, the church renews its covenant to be the body of Christ in the world and to live the life of Christ on behalf of others.

The communion meal is a sign of the unity of believers with one another as the church (1 Cor. 10:17). As branches are part of the vine, so believers are to be united with each other in Christ. Believers are to come to the Lord's table in a worthy manner, without factions among them (1 Cor. 11:17-22, 27-34). Churches are encouraged to find ways to promote reconciliation and to prepare members for communion. The believers' covenant with one another includes the pledge of love for brothers and sisters, of mutual accountability, of confession and forgiveness of sins, and of the sharing of material and spiritual resources as there is need. Such love and sharing reaches around the world as the church recognizes its global unity.

This joyful, yet solemn fellowship in the Lord's Supper is a foretaste of the fuller joy to come when all believers will feast with Christ in the reign of God (Rev. 19:9; compare Isa. 25:6-8).

3. Like baptism, the Lord's Supper is a sign, representing both God's action and covenant faithfulness in delivering us from sin and death, and representing the action of those who re-commit to faithfulness in covenant with God. Because the church's response to God's salvation through Jesus includes thankfulness, the Lord's Supper has sometimes been called "eu-charist," which means "thanksgiving." And because the Lord's Supper represents an event in which Jesus invited the commu-nity of his disciples to share the cup and the bread in fellowship with him and with each other around the same table, it is some-times called "communion."

4. The practice of the early church was to celebrate the Lord's Supper frequently, every Lord's day or even daily (Acts 2:46). The Anabaptists in the sixteenth century also shared the Lord's Supper often as a sign of their renewed covenant with God and each other. Our churches are encouraged to celebrate the Lord's Supper frequently, so that they may participate in the rich meanings of this event for the worship and life of the church.

Article 13
Foot Washing

We believe that Jesus Christ calls us to serve one another in love as he did. Rather than seeking to lord it over others, we are called to follow the example of our Lord, who chose the role of a servant by washing his disciples' feet.

Just before his death, Jesus stooped to wash the disciples' feet and told them, "So if I, your Lord and Teacher, have washed your feet, you also ought to wash one another's feet. For I have given you an example, that you also should do as I have done to you."[1] In this act, Jesus showed humility and servanthood, even laying down his life for those he loved. In washing the disciples' feet, Jesus acted out a parable of his life unto death for them, and of the way his disciples are called to live in the world.

Believers who wash each other's feet show that they share in the body of Christ.[2] They thus acknowledge their frequent need of cleansing, renew their willingness to let go of pride and worldly power, and offer their lives in humble service and sacrificial love.[3]

(1) John 13:14-15. (2) John 13:8. (3) Matt. 20:20-28; Mark 9:30-37; Luke 22:25-27. *who's the greatest*

Commentary

1. Foot washing was common in first-century Palestine, where people wore sandals to walk the dusty roads. Normally, people washed their own feet. Occasionally a disciple would wash the feet of a teacher as an act of extraordinary devotion (see John 12:1-8). No one would have expected Jesus, the master, to wash his disciples' feet.

2. John 13:1-30 recounts Jesus' washing his disciples' feet. The act is followed by a commentary (13:31–17:26), which explains what it meant for Jesus to love his own who were in the world unto the end (13:1), even those who would betray or deny him. His love reached all the way to laying down his life for them (15:13). He laid aside the privileges of power, although "the Father had given all things into his hands" (13:3). He showed the true power that comes through servanthood: "He humbled himself and became obedient to the point of death—even death on a cross. Therefore God also highly exalted him" (Phil. 2:8-9).

Those who follow Jesus are likewise called to let go of privilege and pride in order to love others more fully, even those who are hard to love. By this life of love, they show that they are cleansed and a part of Christ (John 13:8-10). Washing one another's feet is a way of expressing this commitment to follow Jesus in powerful, humble service.

3. Among our congregations, some practice foot washing, while others have discontinued the practice or have never observed it. Congregations are encouraged to practice foot washing when it is a meaningful symbol of service and love for each other. "Washing the feet of the saints" (1 Tim. 5:10) is one way of representing Christ to each other in acts of hospitality, service, and love.

to be a servant you need to be available

Article 14
Discipline in the Church

We believe that the practice of discipline in the church is a sign of God's offer of forgiveness and transforming grace to believers who are moving away from faithful discipleship or who have been overtaken by sin. Discipline is intended to liberate erring brothers and sisters from sin, to enable them to return to a right relationship with God, and to restore them to fellowship in the church. It also gives integrity to the church's witness and contributes to the credibility of the gospel message in the world.

According to the teaching of Jesus Christ and the apostles, all believers participate in the church's mutual care and discipline as appropriate. Jesus gave the church authority to discern right and wrong and to forgive sins when there is repentance or to retain sins when there is no repentance.[1] When becoming members of the church, believers therefore commit themselves to give and receive counsel within the faith community on important matters of doctrine and conduct.

Mutual encouragement, pastoral care, and discipline should normally lead to confession, forgiveness, and reconciliation. Corrective discipline in the church should be exercised in a redemptive manner. The basic pattern begins with "speaking the truth in love," in direct conversation between the erring person and another member.[2] Depending on the person's response, admonition may continue within a broader circle. This usually includes a pastor or congregational leader. If necessary, the matter may finally be brought to the congregation. A brother or sister who repents is to be forgiven and encouraged in making the needed change.

If the erring member persists in sin without repentance and rejects even the admonition of the congregation, membership may be suspended. Suspension of membership is the recognition that persons have separated themselves from the body of Christ.[3] When this occurs, the church continues to pray for them and seeks to restore them to its fellowship.[4]

We acknowledge that discipline, rightly understood and practiced, undergirds the integrity of the church's witness in word and deed. Persistent and uncorrected false teaching and sinful conduct among Christians undermine the proclamation and credibility of the gospel in the world.[5] As a sign of forgiveness and transforming grace, discipline exemplifies the message of forgiveness and new life in Christ through the power of the Holy Spirit. As a means of strengthening good teaching and sustaining moral conduct, it helps to build faithfulness in understanding and practice.

(1) Matt. 18:15-22; John 20:21-23; Gal. 6:1-2; Deut. 19:15. (2) Eph. 4:15; Matt. 18:15. (3) 1 Cor. 5:3-5. (4) 2 Cor. 2:5-11. (5) Matt. 5:14-18; Rom. 2:21ff.

Commentary

1. Anabaptists and Mennonites in sixteenth-century Europe saw discipline as vital for pastoral care and for the well-being of the church. Indeed, they considered discipline to be as important for church renewal as believers baptism and participation in the Lord's Supper.

Mennonites have traditionally emphasized church discipline. Discipline has sometimes been neglected in many Mennonite congregations, in part because of some misuses, in part because of cultural and social influences.

Both the misuse and the neglect of discipline undermine the church's life and witness. Both misuse and neglect work against the important correcting, renewing, and redemptive purposes of church discipline in pastoral care, nurture, and congregational life.

2. In some church traditions, responsibility for church discipline has been limited to particular ministerial offices, such as pastor or bishop. From a Mennonite perspective, discipline is related, first of all, to the mutual care of members for one another. According to the rule of Christ (Matt. 18:15-18), all believers are to offer mutual encouragement, correction, and forgiveness to each other. For that reason, it is good to include a promise to give and receive counsel when persons are received into church membership.

Pastors and other church leaders have a special responsibility to give guidance and to carry out discipline in the life of the church (Acts 20:28-31; Tit. 1:5-11; 1 Pet. 5:1-4; Heb. 13:17). They are to exercise their responsibility lovingly, in gentleness of spirit, and without partiality.

3. Pastors and other church leaders who move away from faithful discipleship or are overtaken by sin are not exempt from discipline in the church. Because of their representative ministries, their teaching and conduct can greatly help or hurt members of the church and the church's witness in the world. They are therefore accountable to the congregation which they serve and to the broader church.

Pastors, teachers, and other church leaders may sometimes be victims of gossip and unjust accusations. Allegations against them should be tested carefully (1 Tim. 5:19). Not only do the failures of ministerial leaders damage the church's life and witness; unfounded accusations against them also do injury to them and the church.

4. The New Testament gives several reasons for suspending fellowship or for excommunication: denying that Jesus Christ

has come in the flesh, persisting in sinful conduct without repentance, and causing divisions in the church by opposing apostolic teaching (for example, 1 John 4:1-6; 1 Cor. 5:1-13; Rom. 16:17-18).

5. For more discussion related to church discipline, see also "Discipleship and the Christian Life" (Article 17) and "Christian Spirituality" (Article 18).

Article 15
Ministry and Leadership

We believe that ministry continues the work of Christ, who gives gifts through the Holy Spirit to all believers and empowers them for service in the church and in the world. We also believe that God calls particular persons in the church to specific leadership ministries and offices. All who minister are accountable to God and to the community of faith as they serve the church.

Christ invites all Christians to minister to each other in the church and on behalf of the church beyond its boundaries.[1] Christ enables them for ministry in response to specific needs and opportunities.[2] Such service is a participation in God's creative work of building up the body of Christ in love and of witnessing to God's righteousness in the world.[3]

The church calls, trains, and appoints gifted men and women to a variety of leadership ministries on its behalf. These may include such offices as pastor, deacon, and elder as well as evangelists, missionaries, teachers, conference ministers, and overseers.[4] The character and reputation of leaders is to be above reproach. Following the example of Christ, persons so appointed preach and teach with authority, interpret the Scriptures and the faith diligently, speak divine truth with boldness, equip the saints, relate with compassion to the needy, and lead the congregation in faithful living, so that the church may be "built together spiritually into a dwelling place for God."[5]

The confirmation of the call to a particular ministry is a sign of mutual accountability between the church and its chosen representative. A time of discernment may be followed by ordination or a similar act, accompanied by laying on of hands.[6] This act symbolizes the person's responsibility as a servant of the Word. The congregation and the wider church or conference share in this act as an indication of their blessing and support and as a reminder of the person's accountability before God and the church, and of the church's responsibility toward the person.

(1) Matt. 25:31-40; 1 Cor. 12:31–13:13. (2) Eph. 4:7; Rom. 12:4-6; 1 Pet. 4:10-11. (3) Eph. 4:15-16; Luke 10:1-37. (4) Eph. 4:11-13; 1 Cor. 12:28; Rom. 12:6-8; 1 Tim. 3:1-13; Tit. 1:5-9. (5) Rom. 10:14-15; Matt. 7:29; Titus 2:15; 1 Tim. 4:13; Jer. 1:4-10; 2 Tim. 4:1-3; Eph. 4:11-13; Phil. 2:1-4; Eph. 2:22. (6) 1 Tim. 5:22; Exod. 29:35.

Commentary

1. The Anabaptists called persons to special roles of spiritual leadership in the church. The study of the Bible, the need for order, and the recognition of giftedness led them to this practice. The purpose of such chosen leaders was not to relieve the other believers of responsibility, but to represent Christ and the church in the congregation and on the church's behalf in the world. The Anabaptists did not use the concept of the "priesthood of all believers" to downplay the need for spiritual leaders with special roles in the church. Menno Simons mentioned the "priesthood of all believers" to encourage all believers, as "priests," to lead a holy life in order to be witnesses to the God who called them from darkness to light (1 Pet. 2:9).

2. In the New Testament the earliest references to leadership ministries mention disciples and apostles. Ephesians 4:11 mentions a fivefold ministry of apostles, prophets, evangelists, pastors, and teachers. In 1 Timothy 3, bishops and deacons are named. We also see a threefold pattern emerging in the New Testament: bishops, elders, and deacons. In the Mennonite tra-

dition this threefold pattern can be found as well. There have also been variations, such as sending out evangelists and missionaries. The church has adapted its leadership patterns from time to time and should have the freedom to continue to do so, including the recognition of evangelists, prophets, and teachers.

3. The act of ordination (or similar acts such as licensing and commissioning) symbolizes a combination of God's call, the congregation's affirmation, the recipient's dedication to ministry, and the blessing of the wider church. Ordination follows a process of discernment in the congregation and in the wider church or conference. It is a one-time event, kept active by continuing service in and for the church. Ordination is normally transferable from one congregation or conference assignment to another. Licensing for pastoral assignments is for a preliminary period of time. Commissioning is normally for a specific assignment.

Article 16
Church Order and Unity

We believe that the church of Jesus Christ is one body with many members, ordered in such a way that, through the one Spirit, believers may be built together spiritually into a dwelling place for God.[1]

As God's people, the church is a holy temple,[2] a spiritual house,[3] founded upon the apostles and prophets, with Christ Jesus himself as the cornerstone.[4] Church order is needed to maintain unity on important matters of faith and life[5] so that each may serve and be served, and the body of Christ may be built up in love.[6] Love and unity in the church are a witness to the world of God's love.[7]

In making decisions, whether to choose leaders or resolve issues, members of the church listen and speak in a spirit of prayerful openness, with the Scriptures as the constant guide. Persons shall expect not only affirmation, but also correction. In a process of discernment, it is better to wait patiently for a word from the Lord leading toward consensus, than to make hasty decisions.

The church is a variety of assemblies which meet regularly, including local congregations and larger conferences. This diversity in unity evokes gratitude to God and appreciation for one another. According to the example of the apostolic church, the local congregation seeks the counsel of the wider church in important matters relating to faith and life, and they work together in their common mission.[8] Decisions made at larger assemblies and conferences are confirmed by constituent groups,[9] and local ministries are encouraged and supported by the wider gatherings. Authority and responsibility are delegated by common and voluntary agreement, so that the churches hold each other accountable to Christ and to one another on all levels of church life.

(1) Eph. 2:21-22. (2) 1 Cor. 3:16-17. (3) 1 Pet. 2:5.
(4) Eph. 2:20. (5) Ps. 133:1; 1 Cor. 14:33; Eph. 4:3.
(6) Eph. 4:7, 12-16. (7) John 17:20-24. (8) Acts 15:1-21.
(9) Acts 11:18.

Commentary

1. Scripture does not prescribe one specific church polity, or government. At the same time, guidelines can be gleaned from both the Old and New Testaments. The priesthood and the temple in Israel's religious life are reminders of the importance of order and also of the concern for visible worship that upholds justice, kindness, and humility (Lev. 8–10; 1 Kings 6). The apostle Paul asked the church to do all things decently and in order to build up the body of Christ (1 Cor. 14:26, 40). The New Testament stresses that the church be organized in a way that encourages participation of all members and the use of their spiritual gifts—for worship, for decision making, for teaching and learning, for mutual care, and for furthering God's mission in the world. The Spirit of Christ leads the church in adapting its organization to the needs of its time and place.

2. Decision making by consensus is a way of coming to unity in the church (see Acts 15:22). Consensus means that the church has together sought for the unity of the Spirit. The church listens carefully to all voices, majority and minority. Consensus is reached when the church has come to one mind on the matter, or when those who dissent have indicated that they do not wish to stand in the way of a group decision. Consensus does not necessarily mean complete unanimity.

3. The church is the assembly of the people of God. The local congregation which meets frequently is the church. Larger conference groups which assemble less often are also the church (1 Thess. 1:1; 1 Pet. 1:1). Church membership involves commitment to a local congregation as well as to a larger church family which may have more than one level of conference affiliation. More broadly, we are united through our common Lord to the universal church, which includes believers in every place and time. We appreciate this wider family of believers and seek to nurture appropriate relationships with them.

Mennonite church structures have upheld the centrality of the church as a community of believers. Some have emphasized the local congregation as the primary unit of the church. Others have seen the wider church (the conference) as the primary unit. The first case reflects a congregation-to-conference polity, where the local congregation determines the extent of its accountability to the larger church. The second has resulted in a conference-to-congregation polity, where the larger church carries more authority. Neither of our Mennonite bodies is clearly on one side or the other. One tendency has been to promote the congregation as the primary unit. This emphasis encourages local initiative, but it can detract from the church's wider mission and from broader church cooperation. The church should be viewed as one seamless garment, extending from the smallest unit ("where two or three are gathered," Matt. 18:20) to the worldwide church. Accountability and responsibility apply to every level of church.

Article 17

Discipleship and the Christian Life

We believe that Jesus Christ calls us to take up our cross and follow him. Through the gift of God's saving grace, we are empowered to be disciples of Jesus, filled with his Spirit, following his teachings and his path through suffering to new life. As by faith we walk in Christ's way, we are being transformed into his image. We become conformed to Christ, faithful to the will of God, and separated from the evil in the world.

The experience of God through the Holy Spirit, prayer, Scripture, and the church empowers us and teaches us how to follow Christ. Likewise, as we follow Christ in our lives, we are brought into closer relationship with God, and Christ dwells in us.[1] Through grace, God works in us to recreate us in the image of Christ, himself the image of the invisible God. Wherever Christian faith is active in love and truth, there is the new creation. By the new birth, we are adopted into God's family, becoming children of God.[2] Our participation in Christ includes both salvation and discipleship.

Conformity to Christ necessarily implies nonconformity to the world.[3] True faith in Christ means willingness to do the will of God, rather than willful pursuit of individual happiness.[4] True faith means seeking first the reign of God in simplicity, rather than pursuing materialism.[5] True faith means acting in peace and justice, rather than with violence or military means.[6] True faith means giving first loyalty to God's kingdom, rather than to any nation-state or ethnic group that claims our allegiance.[7] True faith means honest affirmation of the truth, rather than reliance on oaths to guarantee our truth telling.[8] True faith means chastity and loving faithfulness to marriage vows, rather than the distortion of sexual relationships, contrary to God's intention.[9] True faith means treating our bodies as God's temples, rather than allowing addictive behaviors to take hold. True faith means performing deeds of compassion and reconciliation, in holiness of life, instead of letting sin rule over us.[10] Our faithfulness to Christ is lived out in the loving life and witness of the church community, which is to be a separated people, holy to God.

In all areas of life, we are called to be Jesus' disciples. Jesus is our example, especially in his suffering for the right without retaliation,[11] in his love for enemies, and in his forgiveness of those who persecuted him. Yet, as we follow Jesus, we look not only to the cross, but through the cross, to the joy of the resurrection. We place our hope in God's vindication of those who take the narrow way that leads to life.[12] "If we have died with him, we will also live with him. If we endure, we will also reign with him."[13]

(1) Phil. 3:10. (2) Rom. 8:12-17. (3) Rom. 12:1-2. (4) Matt. 26:39. (5) Matt. 5:3; 6:25-33. (6) Zech. 4:6; Matt. 5:6, 9, 38-48. (7) Josh. 24; Ps. 47; Acts 5:29. (8) Matt. 5:33-37. (9) Matt. 5:27-30. (10) Mic. 6:8; Rom. 6:12-14. (11) 1 Pet. 2:21-23; Rom. 12:9-21. (12) Matt. 7:13-14. (13) 2 Tim. 2:11-12.

Commentary

1. Christians are called to be separate from the evil in the world. Our nonconformity does not mean that we withdraw from all contact with those outside the church. Rather, our way

of thinking is changed, and we avoid sinful behavior and participation in groups which promote sin (Rom. 12:2; 1 Cor. 5:9-10).
When we do not conform to the evil ways of the world, others
will sometimes separate themselves from us (John 3:20). We are
able to be nonconformed to evil when we are conformed to
Christ and willing to let the Holy Spirit transform us into
Christ's image.

2. Suffering may often be the result of discipleship. Jesus
said, "If any want to become my followers, let them deny themselves and take up their cross daily and follow me" (Luke 9:23).
The early Christians also saw persecution for the faith as sharing
in the sufferings of Jesus, who was their example of not repaying
evil for evil (Heb. 2:10; 1 Pet. 3:8-18; 4:12-19). Yet suffering is
not to be sought for its own sake. Jesus healed many who suf-
fered, and it is right to pray for healing and for rescue from evil
(Matt. 6:13). God does not tempt anyone (James 1:13) nor desire
that we suffer, though God can use suffering to instruct us and
bring us to salvation.

Jesus promised blessings for those who suffer for righteousness' sake (Matt. 5:10-12; Luke 9:23-26). The New Testament
understands discipleship as participation in Christ: in his ministry, in his suffering and death, and in his resurrection (for example, 2 Cor. 4:7-12). Those who share in his suffering will also
share his glory. Giving our all for the reign of God brings us joy
(Matt. 13:44-46).

3. Discipleship is to be lived out in the context of Christian
community. As individuals we are called to follow Jesus, and the
church community is also called to a life of discipleship. In the
congregation, discipleship is also closely connected with discipline and mutual care. Christ's disciples together learn how to
follow Christ more nearly in their love for each other and in
their accountability to each other.

4. The articles that follow cover specific aspects of discipleship: "Christian Spirituality" (Article 18), "Family, Singleness,

and Marriage" (Article 19), "Truth and the Avoidance of Oaths" (Article 20), "Christian Stewardship" (Article 21), "Peace, Justice, and Nonresistance" (Article 22), and "The Church's Relation to Government and Society" (Article 23). See also Article 8 "Salvation" for a discussion of faith and faithfulness.

Article 18
Christian Spirituality

We believe that to be a disciple of Jesus is to know life in the Spirit. As we experience relationship with God, the life, death, and resurrection of Jesus Christ take shape in us, and we grow in the image of Christ. In individual and communal worship, the Holy Spirit is present, leading us deeper into the wisdom of God.

By confessing Christ and receiving baptism, we are brought into a new relationship with God through Christ. In God's love, our whole life is freed, transformed, reordered, and renewed. In loving and knowing God, we experience communion with God and allow more and more of our life to be conformed to the way of Jesus—his life, death, and resurrection. We yield ourselves to God, letting the Holy Spirit mold us into the image of Christ.[1] As individual Christians and as the church, we are called to be in relationship with God, reflecting the way of Christ, being filled with the Holy Spirit. We are to grow up in every way into Christ, who is the head of the church, through whom it is built up in love.[2]

We draw the life of the Spirit from Jesus Christ, just as a branch draws life from the vine. Severed from the vine, the power of the Spirit cannot fill us. But as we make our home in Christ and Christ abides in us, we bear fruit and become his disciples.[3] When we are in the presence of the Spirit, we also keep in step with the Spirit and show the fruit of the Spirit in our actions.[4] Our outer behavior matches our inner life.

Spiritual disciplines such as prayer, study of Scripture,

reflection on God, corporate worship, singing hymns, simplicity, witness, and service are training in godliness.[5] Such disciplines open us to a growing relationship with God and to putting ourselves more completely into the hands of God. Disciplines are also preparation for times of testing and of suffering. If we practice the presence of God in calmer times, we find it easier to know God's presence in difficult times.

We are convinced that nothing can separate us from the love of God in Christ Jesus our Lord,[6] for God can use both joy and suffering to nurture our spiritual growth.[7] In this age, Christ in us is our hope of glory.[8] We look forward to that time when our partial knowledge of God will become complete, and we will see face to face.[9]

(1) 2 Cor. 3:17-18; Phil. 3:21. (2) Eph. 4:15-16. (3) John 15:5-8. (4) Ps. 1; Gal. 5:22-26. (5) 1 Tim. 4:7-8. (6) Rom. 8:35-39. (7) Matt. 5:1-12; Ps. 119:67. (8) Col. 1:27. (9) 1 Cor. 13:12.

Commentary

1. *Spirituality* is a relatively recent term used to refer to life in the Spirit and the experience of God. Anabaptists and Mennonites have used several words to describe spirituality, such as piety, humility, *Gelassenheit* (yieldedness or letting go), *Frömmigkeit* (piety), and *Nachfolge* (following Christ). These concepts all have to do with radical openness to knowing God and to doing God's will. They do not separate spirituality from ethics, or reflection from action. For this reason, this confession of faith includes spirituality in the section on discipleship. Jesus taught that the pure (or clean) in heart are the ones who will see God (Matt. 5:8).

2. Many religious traditions speak of spirituality, or experience of the divine. People sometimes claim that all such experi-

ences are really the same. But at least two distinct streams can be identified in the history of Christian spirituality. In the stream influenced primarily by Greek philosophy, the goal is *union* with God, the individual's absorption into God. Loving the neighbor and following Christ are by-products of this union with God.

The second stream is influenced more by biblical thought. The goal of its action and contemplation is *communion* with God, or covenant relationship with God. It is more focused on Jesus Christ—his life, death, and resurrection—as the way for believers. The Anabaptists of the sixteenth century were not the first to recognize that knowing Christ and following Christ in life are interwoven; many earlier dissenters had also connected spiritual insight with ethics. This confession of faith identifies more strongly with the second stream by affirming that Christian spirituality is defined by Christ and his way, in accordance with the Scriptures.

3. The Holy Spirit is present to God's people individually and corporately. The New Testament refers to both the gathered body and the individual Christian as a temple or dwelling place for the Holy Spirit (1 Cor. 3:16-17; Eph. 2:21-22; 1 Cor. 6:19). Both personal devotion and corporate worship, individual action and community activity, are occasions for the Spirit's work in, among, and through us.

4. The list of spiritual disciplines mentioned in this article is not complete. Fasting, keeping a journal, alms giving, and other disciplines could have been included. Practicing the spiritual disciplines is good in itself, and it produces other desirable results. Scripture study leads us toward knowing God, as well as increasing our knowledge about God. Worship contributes to our spiritual growth, as well as declaring our praise and our allegiance to God. Giving alms helps us to seek the kingdom of God by keeping us from becoming too attached to material things, as well as helping the poor.

Family, Singleness, and Marriage

We believe that God intends human life to begin in families and to be blessed through families. Even more, God desires all people to become part of the church, God's family. As single and married members of the church family give and receive nurture and healing, Christian family relationships can grow toward the wholeness that God intends.

We recognize that God has created human beings for relationship. God intends human life to be blessed through families, especially through the family of faith. All Christians are to take their place within the household of God, where members treat each other as brothers and sisters.[1] We hold that within the church family, the goodness of being either single or married is honored.[2] We honor the single state and encourage the church to respect and to include single persons in the life and activities of the church family. Families of faith are called to be a blessing to all families of the earth.[3]

We believe that God intends marriage to be a covenant between one man and one woman for life.[4] Christian marriage is a mutual relationship in Christ,[5] a covenant made in the context of the church. According to Scripture, right sexual union takes place only within the marriage relationship.[6] Marriage is meant for sexual intimacy, companionship, and the birth and nurture of children.

Children are of great importance. Jesus saw them as examples of how to receive the reign of God.[7] Children are to be loved, disciplined, taught, and respected in the home and in the church. Children are also to honor their parents, obeying them in the Lord.[8] Younger people are to respect their elders in the home and the church.[9]

The church is called to help couples strengthen their marriage relationship and to encourage reconciliation in times of conflict. The church is also to minister with truth and compassion to persons in difficult family relationships. As the family of God, the church is called to be a sanctuary offering hope and healing for families.

(1) Ps. 27:10; Luke 8:19-21; Eph. 2:19. (2) 1 Cor. 7:38.
(3) Gen. 12:1-3; Acts 3:25. (4) Mark 10:9; 1 Cor. 7:10-11.
(5) Eph. 5:21. (6) Exod. 20:14; 1 Cor. 6:12-20. (7) Mark 10:13-16. (8) Exod. 20:12; Eph. 6:1-4. (9) 1 Tim. 5:1-2.

Commentary

1. Although *family* generally refers to relationships of blood, marriage, or adoption, the Scripture also describes the church as a family. Especially common in the New Testament are the references to Christians as brothers and sisters and as children of God (see Rom. 8:12-17; Gal. 4:5-7; James 2:15).

2. Many in the church remain single or become single. Jesus encouraged some to choose a life of singleness for the sake of the reign of God (Matt. 19:12; Luke 14:20). While Paul regarded marriage as a positive choice, he preferred voluntary singleness for the sake of unconditional commitment to the Lord (1 Cor. 7:25-35).

3. Scripture places sexual intimacy within God's good created order (Gen. 2:23-25). Sexual union is reserved for the marriage bond (Exod. 20:14; Mark 10:11; Rom. 7:1-3). Sexual union is for pleasure and closeness and for procreation. Through procreation, the human family continues from generation to generation. The oneness between husband and wife is a mystery which reflects the oneness of the Godhead and the oneness between

Christ and his church. We affirm that Christians who marry should marry in the Lord, to a Christian spouse.

4. Some in the church experience divorce, abuse, sexual misconduct, and other problems that make marriage and family life burdensome or even impossible. Jesus affirmed the sanctity of marriage (Matt. 5:32) and pointed to hardness of the heart as the ultimate cause of divorce (Mark 10:4-9). Today's church needs to uphold the permanency of marriage and help couples in conflict move toward reconciliation. At the same time, the church, as a reconciling and forgiving community, offers healing and new beginnings. The church is to bring strength and healing to individuals and families.

Nov. 7

Article 20
Truth and the Avoidance of Oaths

We commit ourselves to tell the truth, to give a simple yes or no, and to avoid swearing of oaths.

Jesus told his disciples not to swear oaths at all, but to let their yes be yes, and their no be no.[1] We believe that this teaching applies to truth telling as well as to avoiding profane language.[2] An oath is often sworn as a guarantee that one is telling the truth. This implies that when one has not taken an oath, one may be less careful about telling the truth. Jesus' followers are always to speak the truth and, in legal matters, simply to affirm that their statements are true.

Jesus also warned against using oaths to try to compel God to guarantee the future. In faith, we commit our futures to God.[3]

Throughout history, human governments have asked citizens to swear oaths of allegiance. As Christians, our first allegiance is to God.[4] In baptism we pledged our loyalty to Christ's community, a commitment that takes precedence over obedience to any other social and political communities.

(1) Matt. 5:33-37; James 5:12. (2) Eph. 4:15, 29. (3) Matt. 5:34-36. (4) Acts 5:29.

Commentary

1. In the biblical languages, *truth* is related to faithfulness—faithfulness to the facts (speaking truth) as well as faithfulness in relationships (being true). Speaking the truth in love in the

Christian community shows our commitment to right relationships as well as to accurate speech.

2. We follow the Anabaptist-Mennonite tradition, which has usually applied Jesus' words against taking oaths in these ways: in affirming rather than swearing in courts of law and in other legal matters, in a commitment to unconditional truth telling and to keeping one's word, in avoiding membership in oath-bound or secret societies, in refusing to take oaths of allegiance that would conflict with our ultimate allegiance to God through Christ, and in avoiding all profane oaths.

Jesus' counsel to tell the truth without oaths and to be true in our relationships applies to family life, business dealings, advertising, and other agreements we make.

Article 21
Christian Stewardship

We believe that everything belongs to God, who calls us as the church to live as faithful stewards of all that God has entrusted to us.

As servants of God, our primary vocation is to be stewards in God's household.[1] God, who in Christ has given us new life, has also given us spiritual gifts to use for the church's nurture and mission.[2] The message of reconciliation has been entrusted to every believer, so that through the church the mystery of the gospel might be made known to the world.[3]

We believe that time also belongs to God and that we are to use with care the time of which we are stewards.[4] Yet, from earliest days, the people of God have been called to observe special periods of rest and worship. In the Old Testament, the seventh day was holy because it was the day God rested from the work of creation.[5] The Sabbath was also holy because of God's deliverance of the Hebrew people from slavery.[6] Through Jesus, all time is holy, set apart for God and intended to be used for salvation, healing, and justice.[7] In the present time, the church celebrates a day of holy rest, commonly the first day of the week, and is called to live according to Sabbath justice at all times.

We acknowledge that God as Creator is owner of all things. In the Old Testament, the Sabbath year and the Jubilee year were practical expressions of the belief that the land is God's and the people of Israel belong to God.[8] Jesus, at the beginning of his ministry, announced the year of the Lord's favor, often identified with Jubilee. Through

Jesus, the poor heard good news, captives were released, the blind saw, and the oppressed went free.[9] The first church in Jerusalem put Jubilee into practice by preaching the gospel, healing the sick, and sharing possessions. Other early churches shared financially with those in need.[10]

As stewards of God's earth, we are called to care for the earth and to bring rest and renewal to the land and everything that lives on it.[11] As stewards of money and possessions, we are to live simply, practice mutual aid within the church, uphold economic justice, and give generously and cheerfully.[12] As persons dependent on God's providence, we are not to be anxious about the necessities of life, but to seek first the kingdom of God.[13] We cannot be true servants of God and let our lives be ruled by desire for wealth.

We are called to be stewards in the household of God, set apart for the service of God. We live out now the rest and justice which God has promised.[14] The church does this while looking forward to the coming of our Master and the restoration of all things in the new heaven and new earth.

(1) Luke 12:35-48; 1 Cor. 4:1-2. (2) 1 Pet. 4:10-11; Tit. 1:7; 2:5. (3) 2 Cor. 5:18-20; Eph. 3:1-10. (4) Ps. 31:15; Eph. 5:15-16; Col. 4:5. (5) Exod. 20:8-11. (6) Deut. 5:12-15. (7) Mark 2:27-28. (8) Lev. 25:23, 42, 55. (9) Luke 4:16-21. (10) Acts 2:44-45; 4:32-37; 2 Cor. 8:1-15. (11) Ps. 24:1; Gen. 1:26-28. (12) Phil. 4:11-12; 2 Cor. 8:13-14; James 5:4; 2 Cor. 9:7. (13) Matt. 6:24-33. (14) Matt. 11:28-29; Rev. 7:15-17.

Commentary

1. The word *stewardship* in the New Testament is used primarily in connection with stewardship of the gospel. But in the

broader sense, stewardship is related to the idea of God as head of the household, in which Christians are God's servants or managers or sons and daughters entrusted with responsibility. First-century households acted as economic units and often included people not biologically related. Thus, the term *stewardship* has come to refer to our responsibility both for sharing the gospel and for managing time, material things, and money.

2. Our tradition of simple living is rooted not in frugality for its own sake, but in dependence on God, the owner of everything, for our material needs. We depend on God's gracious gifts for food and clothing, for our salvation, and for life itself. We do not need to hold on tightly to money and possessions, but can share what God has given us. The practice of mutual aid is a part of sharing God's gifts so that no one in the family of faith will be without the necessities of life. Whether through community of goods or other forms of financial sharing, mutual aid continues the practice of Israel in giving special care to widows, orphans, aliens, and others in economic need (Deut. 24:17-22). Tithes and first-fruit offerings were also a part of this economic sharing (Deut. 26; compare Matt. 23:23).

3. Economic justice is an integral part of the Sabbath cycle. The Sabbath year, like the Sabbath day, brought rest and freedom for the land and for laborers. The seven-times-seventh year or the fiftieth year, the year of Jubilee, also brought justice and mercy by the return of family land, release of debts, and freedom for bound laborers (Lev. 25). The effect of the Sabbath-Jubilee laws was a return to relative economic equality every fifty years. Jesus taught his disciples to pray, "Forgive us our debts, as we also have forgiven our debtors" (Matt. 6:12). In the age to come, the saints will have the economic necessities (Rev. 7:15-17). We are to seek first the reign of God and to cease from consumerism, unchecked competition, overburdened productivity, greed, and possessiveness.

4. Not only was the Sabbath observed in Old Testament times; there is evidence that the sabbatical year and the year of Jubilee were also observed. Jubilee law appears in Leviticus 25; Leviticus 27:16-25; and Numbers 36:4. Other references to sabbatical or Jubilee years occur in Deuteronomy 31:10; 2 Chronicles 36:21; Isaiah 37:30; 61:1-2; Jeremiah 34:8-22; and Ezekiel 46:17. The first-century Jewish historian Josephus refers to a time when the Jews in Palestine went hungry because of a sabbatical or Jubilee year, when the land lay fallow. The Roman government exempted Judea from tribute during the seventh year. The practice of the Jerusalem church and the continued financial sharing of Christian congregations is evidence that the economic aspects of Jubilee continued to be practiced and adapted to urban settings.

5. The theology of stewardship makes us aware not only of care for human beings, but of care for the rest of creation. Animals and fields benefited from the Sabbath and the sabbatical year. An observance of Sabbath-Jubilee calls us to take care of and preserve the earth. We are to commit ourselves to right use of the earth's resources as a way of living now according to the model of the new heaven and the new earth.

Article 22
Peace, Justice, and Nonresistance

We believe that peace is the will of God. God created the world in peace, and God's peace is most fully revealed in Jesus Christ, who is our peace and the peace of the whole world. Led by the Holy Spirit, we follow Christ in the way of peace, doing justice, bringing reconciliation, and practicing nonresistance even in the face of violence and warfare.

Although God created a peaceable world, humanity chose the way of unrighteousness and violence.[1] The spirit of revenge increased, and violence multiplied, yet the original vision of peace and justice did not die.[2] Prophets and other messengers of God continued to point the people of Israel toward trust in God rather than in weapons and military force.[3]

The peace God intends for humanity and creation was revealed most fully in Jesus Christ. A joyous song of peace announced Jesus' birth.[4] Jesus taught love of enemies, forgave wrongdoers, and called for right relationships.[5] When threatened, he chose not to resist, but gave his life freely.[6] By his death and resurrection, he has removed the dominion of death and given us peace with God.[7] Thus he has reconciled us to God and has entrusted to us the ministry of reconciliation.[8]

As followers of Jesus, we participate in his ministry of peace and justice. He has called us to find our blessing in making peace and seeking justice. We do so in a spirit of gentleness, willing to be persecuted for righteousness' sake.[9] As disciples of Christ, we do not prepare for war, or participate in war or military service. The same Spirit that empowered Jesus also empowers us to love enemies, to forgive rather than to seek revenge, to practice right relationships, to rely on the community of faith to settle disputes, and to resist evil without violence.[10]

Led by the Spirit, and beginning in the church, we witness to all people that violence is not the will of God. We witness against all forms of violence, including war among nations, hostility among races and classes, abuse of children and women, violence between men and women, abortion, and capital punishment.

We give our ultimate loyalty to the God of grace and peace, who guides the church daily in overcoming evil with good, who empowers us to do justice, and who sustains us in the glorious hope of the peaceable reign of God.[11]

(1) Gen. 1–11. (2) Isa. 2:2-4. (3) Lev. 26:6; Isa. 31:1; Hos. 2:18. (4) Luke 2:14. (5) Matt. 5:44; 6:14-15. (6) Matt. 26:52-53; 1 Pet. 2:21-24. (7) 1 Cor. 15:54-55; Rom. 5:10-11; Eph. 2:11-18. (8) 2 Cor. 5:18-21. (9) Matt. 5:3-12. (10) Matt. 5:39; 1 Cor. 6:1-16; Rom. 12:14-21. (11) Isa. 11:1-9.

Commentary

1. The biblical concept of peace embraces personal peace with God, peace in human relations, peace among nations, and peace with God's creation. The Old Testament word for peace (shalom) includes healing, reconciliation, and well-being. Peace is more than the absence of war; it includes the restoration of right relationship.

Justice and peace belong together, since right relationship involves both. According to Greek and Roman ideas of justice, people should get what they deserve. According to the Bible, justice involves healing and restoring relationships. That is a reason for the special concern for the poor and the oppressed evident in the Bible (Deut. 24:10-22; Matt. 20:1-16; James 2:5).

Nonresistance means "not resisting." Our example is Jesus, who endured accusation and abuse without retaliating. Jesus did sometimes confront wrongdoers (Matt. 23:1-36; John 2:13-22), but he did so in a nonviolent way that shows us how to overcome evil with good (Rom. 12:21; see 1 Pet. 2:21-24).

2. Peace and justice are not optional teachings, counsel that Christians can take or leave. They belong to the heart of gospel message. Sometimes the Mennonite peace position has been based only on the teachings of Jesus. A biblical understanding of peace is also based on the atoning sacrifice of Christ: the atonement is the foundation for our peace with God (Rom. 5:10) and with one another (Eph. 2:13-16).

Similarly, justice is based not only on Jesus' teachings (Luke 4:18-19), but also on his atoning death. Jesus' death on the cross accomplished justice. His crucifixion brought forgiveness and thus restored sinners to right relationship with God. On the cross Jesus cried out to God on behalf of a world mired in sinful, unjust relationships. This cry was amplified by the shedding of his blood, which creates a just, forgiving community of the new covenant (Heb. 5:7-10).

3. In continuity with previous Mennonite confessions of faith, we affirm that nonparticipation in warfare involves conscientious objection to military service and a nonresistant response to violence. Our peace witness also includes peacemaking and working for justice. Peace witness is needed even when the nations in which we live are not at war. Ministries of mediation, conciliation, and nonviolent resolution of everyday conflict can express our commitment to Christ's way of peace.

4. There is no simple explanation for the practice of war in the Old Testament. The Old Testament repeatedly points to-

ward peace (Exod. 14:13-14; Judg. 7:2; Ps. 37; Isa. 31; Hos. 2:18). Both the Old and New Testaments proclaim the vision of a coming peaceable kingdom (Isa. 9:1-7), preached and revealed by Jesus Christ (Acts 10:36).

Article 23

The Church's Relation to Government and Society

We believe that the church is God's "holy nation,"[1] called to give full allegiance to Christ its head and to witness to all nations about God's saving love.

The church is the spiritual, social, and political body that gives its allegiance to God alone. As citizens of God's kingdom,[2] we trust in the power of God's love for our defense. The church knows no geographical boundaries and needs no violence for its protection. The only Christian nation is the church of Jesus Christ, made up of people from every tribe and nation,[3] called to witness to God's glory.

In contrast to the church, governing authorities of the world have been instituted by God for maintaining order in societies. Such governments and other human institutions as servants of God are called to act justly and provide order.[4] But like all such institutions, nations tend to demand total allegiance. They then become idolatrous and rebellious against the will of God.[5] Even at its best, a government cannot act completely according to the justice of God because no nation, except the church, confesses Christ's rule as its foundation.

As Christians we are to respect those in authority and to pray for all people, including those in government, that they also may be saved and come to the knowledge of the truth.[6] We may participate in government or other institutions of society only in ways that do not violate the love and holiness taught by Christ and do not compromise our loyalty to Christ. We witness to the nations by being that "city on a hill" which demonstrates the way of Christ.[7] We also witness by being ambassadors for Christ,[8] calling the nations (and all persons and institutions) to move toward justice, peace, and compassion for all people. In so doing, we seek the welfare of the city to which God has sent us.[9]

We understand that Christ, by his death and resurrection, has won victory over the powers, including all governments.[10] Because we confess that Jesus Christ has been exalted as Lord of lords, we recognize no other authority's claims as ultimate.

(1) 1 Pet. 2:9. (2) Phil. 3:20; Eph. 2:19. (3) Rev. 7:9. (4) Rom. 13:1-7. (5) Ezek. 28; Daniel 7-8; Rev. 13. (6) 1 Tim. 2:1-4. (7) Matt. 5:13-16; Isa. 49:6. (8) 2 Cor. 5:20. (9) Jer. 29:7. (10) Col. 2:15.

Commentary

1. The language of the church as "holy nation" may be unfamiliar. Often, we have spiritualized the political language of the New Testament, forgetting that *kingdom, Lord,* and even the Greek word for *church* (literally, "assembly" or "town meeting") are political words. Political here refers to any structuring of group relationships. Understanding the church as nation can make clearer its relationship to the nations of the world.

Before the fourth century, about the time of the Roman emperor Constantine, most Christians thought of themselves as God's nation, made up of both Jewish and Gentile believers, living among the nations, yet strangers among them (1 Pet. 2:11-17; Heb. 11:13-16). When Christianity became the state religion, the emperor came to be seen as the protector of the faith (even by violence). Church membership was no longer voluntary. Mission efforts were primarily directed toward people outside the empire. Even now, in places where Christianity is no longer the state religion, the government is often seen as the defender of religion, and the church is expected to support government policies.

We believe that Christ is Lord over all of life. Church and state are separate and often competing structures vying for our loyalty. We understand that governments can preserve order and that we owe honor to people in government. But our "fear" belongs to God alone (1 Pet. 2:17). When the demands of the government conflict with the demands of Christ, Christians are to "obey God rather than any human authority" (Acts 5:29).

2. God has one will for all people: salvation and incorporation into the people of God. Territorial nations and their governments are limited in their ability to fulfill the will of God because of their reliance on violence, at least as a last resort, and because of their tendency to try to set themselves up in the place of God. However, a government that acts with relative justice and provides order is better than anarchy or an unjust, oppressive government. Christians may often witness to the state, asking it to act according to higher values or to standards which, while less than what God expects of the church, may bring the state closer to doing the will of God. Christians are responsible to witness to governments not only because of their citizenship in a particular country, but also in order to reflect Christ's compassion for all people and to proclaim Christ's lordship over all human institutions.

3. On a variety of political and social issues, individual Christians need the church to help them discern how to be in the world without belonging to the world (John 17:14-19). The church asks questions such as these: Will this participation in the government or in other institutions of society enable us to be ambassadors of Christ's reconciliation? Or will such participation violate our commitment to the way of Christ and compromise our loyalty to Christ? We ask these questions when we confront issues of military service, office holding, government employment, voting, taxes, participating in the economic system,

using the secular courts, pledging allegiance, using flags, public and private schooling, and seeking to influence legislation. For related discussion, see "Discipleship and the Christian Life" (Article 17), "Peace, Justice, and Nonresistance" (Article 22), and "Truth and the Avoidance of Oaths" (Article 20).

Article 24
The Reign of God

We place our hope in the reign of God and in its fulfillment in the day when Christ our ascended Lord will come again in glory to judge the living and the dead. He will gather his church, already living under the reign of God according to the pattern of God's future. We believe in God's final victory, in the end of this present age of struggle between good and evil, in the resurrection of the dead, and in the appearance of a new heaven and a new earth. There the people of God will reign with Christ in justice, righteousness, and peace.

We believe that God, who created the universe, continues to rule over it in wisdom, patience, and justice, though sinful creation has not yet recognized God's rule. Faithful Israel acclaimed God as king and looked forward to the fullness of God's kingdom.[1] We affirm that, in Jesus' ministry, death, and resurrection, the time of fulfillment has begun.[2] Jesus proclaimed both the nearness of God's reign and its future realization, its healing and its judgment. In his life and teaching, he showed that God's reign included the poor, outcasts, the persecuted, those who were like children, and those with faith like a mustard seed.[3] For this kingdom, God has appointed Jesus Christ as king and Lord.[4]

We believe that the church is called to live now according to the model of the future reign of God. Thus, we are given a foretaste of the kingdom that God will one day establish in full. The church is to be a spiritual, social, and economic reality,[5] demonstrating now the justice, righteousness, love, and peace of the age to come. The church does this in obedience to its Lord and in anticipation that the kingdom of this world will become the kingdom of our Lord.[6]

We believe that, just as God raised Jesus from the dead, we also will be raised from the dead.[7] At Christ's glorious coming again for judgment, the dead will come out of their graves"—those who have done good, to the resurrection of life, and those who have done evil, to the resurrection of condemnation."[8] The righteous will rise to eternal life with God, and the unrighteous to hell and separation from God. Thus, God will bring justice to the persecuted and will confirm the victory over sin, evil, and death itself.

We look forward to the coming of a new heaven and a new earth, and a new Jerusalem, where the people of God will no longer hunger, thirst, or cry,[9] but will sing praises: "To the One seated on the throne and to the Lamb be blessing and honor and glory and might forever and ever! Amen!"[10]

(1) Exod. 15:8; Judg. 8:23; Zech. 14:9. (2) Mark 1:15. (3) Matt. 5:10; 8:10-12; 17:20; 21:31; Luke 6:20. (4) Ps. 2:7; Mark 1:11; Phil. 2:9. (5) Acts 2:41-47. (6) Rev. 11:15; 15:3-4. (7) 1 Cor. 15:12-58. (8) John 5:28-29. (9) Rev. 21:1-4; 7:9-17. (10) Rev. 5:13-14.

Commentary

1. The church is called to live now under the rule of God as a witness to the reign of God. Our life together now is to be patterned after our life together in the age to come. This means that the reign of God is relevant to this world, and the ethics of God's rule should not be postponed to some future time. Yet the church is not identical with the kingdom, or reign, of God. Nor must the church harbor illusions that it can bring about the king-

dom fully in the present age, either all at once or by gradually improving conditions in this world.

2. For some, the idea of God's final judgment is problematic, because it seems to emphasize God's wrath at the expense of God's love and mercy. God's loving patience is so great that God will not coerce anyone into covenant relationship, but will allow those who reject it to remain separated from God. Moreover, God's justice means that unrepentant evildoers will not go unpunished. Those who are suffering for righteousness' sake can look forward to the coming reign of God as a time of vindication and rescue from evil (Ps. 37; Rev. 6:9-11). In the age to come, there will be surprising reversals as the powerful are brought down and the lowly lifted up (Luke 1:52-53; see also Luke 3:5).

This justice for God's people involves the resurrection of the dead and eternal life for those who believe in Christ (John 6:40; 11:25-26). Just as God raised Jesus from the dead, so those who belong to Christ will be raised from death to life (1 Cor. 15:15-21). Now we follow Christ in our mortal bodies; we look forward to life in Christ with new, resurrected bodies (1 Cor. 15:35-57).

The New Testament says much about the resurrection. It speaks much less frequently and clearly about the state of persons between the time of their deaths and the resurrection. Yet, we who are in Christ are assured that not even death can separate us from the love of God (Rom. 8:38-39).

3. Both in the present age and in the age to come, the city of God has a political and social aspect. It is a corporate body, ruled by God through Christ its Lord. Even in the age to come, the city of God is not a disembodied spiritual entity, but participates in the new earth as well as the new heaven. See "The Church's Relation to Government and Society" (Article 23).

Jesus counseled his followers against trying to set dates for the coming age (Matt. 24:36). We should also be cautious about too narrowly identifying persons, places, or events of the end times with particular people, places, and happenings of the present. Instead, God's people should always live in righteousness, praising God, following Christ, led by the Spirit, awaiting in hope the coming of our Lord and Savior Jesus Christ.

Confession of Faith in a Mennonite Perspective

1. We believe that **God** exists and is pleased with all who draw near by faith. We worship the one holy and loving God who is Father, Son, and Holy Spirit eternally. God has created all things visible and invisible, has brought salvation and new life to humanity through Jesus Christ, and continues to sustain the church and all things until the end of the age.

2. We believe in **Jesus Christ**, the Word of God become flesh. He is the Savior of the world, who has delivered us from the dominion of sin and reconciled us to God by his death on a cross. He was declared to be Son of God by his resurrection from the dead. He is the head of the church, the exalted Lord, the Lamb who was slain, coming again to reign with God in glory.

3. We believe in the **Holy Spirit**, the eternal Spirit of God, who dwelled in Jesus Christ, who empowers the church, who is the source of our life in Christ, and who is poured out on those who believe as the guarantee of redemption.

4. We believe that all **Scripture** is inspired by God through the Holy Spirit for instruction in salvation and training in righteousness. We accept the Scriptures as the Word of God and as the fully reliable and trustworthy standard for Christian faith and life. Led by the Holy Spirit in the

church, we interpret Scripture in harmony with Jesus Christ.

5. We believe that God has **created the heavens and the earth** and all that is in them, and that God preserves and renews what has been made. All creation has its source outside itself and belongs to the Creator. The world has been created good because God is good and provides all that is needed for life.

6. We believe that God has **created human beings** in the divine image. God formed them from the dust of the earth and gave them a special dignity among all the works of creation. Human beings have been made for relationship with God, to live in peace with each other, and to take care of the rest of creation.

7. We confess that, beginning with Adam and Eve, humanity has disobeyed God, given way to the tempter, and chosen to **sin**. All have fallen short of the Creator's intent, marred the image of God in which they were created, disrupted order in the world, and limited their love for others. Because of sin, humanity has been given over to the enslaving powers of evil and death.

8. We believe that, through Jesus Christ, God offers **salvation** from sin and a new way of life. We receive God's salvation when we repent and accept Jesus Christ as Savior and Lord. In Christ, we are reconciled with God and brought into the reconciling community. We place our faith in God that, by the same power that raised Christ from the dead, we may be saved from sin to follow Christ and to know the fullness of salvation.

9. We believe that the **church** is the assembly of those who have accepted God's offer of salvation through faith in Jesus Christ. It is the new community of disciples sent into the world to proclaim the reign of God and to provide a foretaste of the church's glorious hope. It is the new society established and sustained by the Holy Spirit.

10. We believe that the **mission** of the church is to proclaim and to be a sign of the kingdom of God. Christ has commissioned the church to make disciples of all nations, baptizing them, and teaching them to observe all things he has commanded.

11. We believe that the **baptism** of believers with water is a sign of their cleansing from sin. Baptism is also a pledge before the church of their covenant with God to walk in the way of Jesus Christ through the power of the Holy Spirit. Believers are baptized into Christ and his body by the Spirit, water, and blood.

12. We believe that the **Lord's Supper** is a sign by which the church thankfully remembers the new covenant which Jesus established by his death. In this communion meal, the church renews its covenant with God and with each other and participates in the life and death of Jesus Christ, until he comes.

13. We believe that in **washing** the **feet** of his disciples, Jesus calls us to serve one another in love as he did. Thus we acknowledge our frequent need of cleansing, renew our willingness to let go of pride and worldly power, and offer our lives in humble service and sacrificial love.

14. We practice **discipline** in the church as a sign of God's offer of transforming grace. Discipline is intended to liberate erring brothers and sisters from sin, and to restore them to a right relationship with God and to fellowship in the church. The practice of discipline gives integrity to the church's witness in the world.

15. We believe that **ministry** is a continuation of the work of Christ, who gives gifts through the Holy Spirit to all believers and empowers them for service in the church and in the world. We also believe that God calls particular persons in the church to specific leadership ministries and offices. All who minister are accountable to God and to the community of faith.

16. We believe that the church of Jesus Christ is **one body** with many members, ordered in such a way that, through the one Spirit, believers may be built together spiritually into a dwelling place for God.

17. We believe that Jesus Christ calls us to **discipleship**, to take up our cross and follow him. Through the gift of God's saving grace, we are empowered to be disciples of Jesus, filled with his Spirit, following his teachings and his path through suffering to new life. As we are faithful to his way, we become conformed to Christ and separated from the evil in the world.

18. We believe that to be a disciple of Jesus is to know **life in the Spirit**. As the life, death, and resurrection of Jesus Christ takes shape in us, we grow in the image of Christ and in our relationship with God. The Holy Spirit is active in individual and in communal worship, leading us deeper into the experience of God.

19. We believe that God intends human life to begin in **families** and to be blessed through families. Even more, God desires all people to become part of the church, God's family. As single and married members of the church family give and receive nurture and healing, families can grow toward the wholeness that God intends. We are called to chastity and to loving faithfulness in marriage.

20. We commit ourselves to tell the **truth**, to give a simple yes or no, and to avoid the swearing of oaths.

21. We believe that everything belongs to God, who calls the church to live in faithful **stewardship** of all that God has entrusted to us, and to participate now in the rest and justice which God has promised.

22. We believe that **peace** is the will of God. God created the world in peace, and God's peace is most fully revealed in Jesus Christ, who is our peace and the peace of the whole world. Led by the Holy Spirit, we follow Christ in the way of peace, doing justice, bringing reconciliation, and practicing nonresistance, even in the face of violence and warfare.

23. We believe that the church is God's holy nation, called to give full allegiance to Christ its head and to witness to every **nation, government, and society** about God's saving love.

24. We place our hope in the **reign of God** and its fulfillment in the day when Christ will come again in glory to judge the living and the dead. He will gather his church, which is already living under the reign of God. We await God's final victory, the end of this present age of struggle,

the resurrection of the dead, and a new heaven and a new earth. There the people of God will reign with Christ in justice, righteousness, and peace for ever and ever.

Unison Reading A

We believe in God the Creator of all,
who has called forth a people of faith.
We believe in Jesus Christ, the Word become flesh,
crucified and resurrected for us.
He is our Savior from evil and sin,
our peace and the exalted Lord of the church.
And we believe in the Holy Spirit,
the source of redemption and life.

We who respond to Christ in faith are his church,
the community called to proclaim
and to be a sign of the kingdom of God,
the new people sustained by Scripture and Spirit.
Thus we continue the mission of Christ,
making disciples, forgiving, restoring,
baptizing believers, sharing the Lord's Supper,
using our gifts in unity and love.

We commit ourselves to follow Jesus Christ,
in his path through suffering to life.
By grace we are being changed into the image of God,
in which God created women and men.
As faithful disciples, we hear Christ's call
to life in the Spirit in relation with God,
to chastity, stewardship, love for the enemy,
to the practice of justice and peace.

We joyfully worship the three-in-one God,
as a holy nation, the people of God,
giving allegiance to Christ as our Lord,
living now as if in the age to come.
We place our hope in God's everlasting reign,
in victory over evil, the resurrection of the dead,
in Christ's coming again in judgment and glory.
To God be all glory! Amen!

Note: This unison reading was written with a fairly regular meter in order to make it suitable to be set to music and sung.

Unison Reading B

We believe in God,
Creator and Sustainer of the universe,
who in love and holiness has called forth a people of faith,
who has spoken to us in Jesus Christ,
 the Word of God become flesh,
  in whom Scripture has its center,
 the one crucified, resurrected,
  and exalted for our sake,
 our Savior from the dominion of sin and evil,
 our peace and our reconciliation,
 our Lord and the head of the church,
 through whom God sends the Holy Spirit,
the source of our life and the guarantee
  of our redemption.

We renew our covenant in Christ's church,
the new community called to proclaim
  and to be a sign of the reign of God,
the assembly of those who have responded in faith
  to Jesus Christ,
the society established and sustained by the Holy Spirit,
 to interpret Scripture, the trustworthy standard
  for faith and life,
 to carry on Jesus' ministry in word and deed,
 to call for repentance and make disciples
  of all peoples,
 to baptize believers and to share the Lord's Supper,
 to offer God's forgiveness and restoration
  to those who sin,

to use our gifts and abilities for God's service,
to live in mutual love, order, and unity,
so that the church may become one new humanity,
        a light to the world.

We commit ourselves to follow Jesus Christ
in his path through suffering to new life,
        relying on the power of the Holy Spirit
            and the gift of God's grace,
        becoming conformed to Christ rather than to evil
            in the world,
        being transformed into the divine image in which
            humanity was created.
As Christ's community of disciples, faithful
        to his covenant, we are called
        to life in the Spirit and relationship with God
            through Christ,
        to chastity and loving faithfulness to marriage vows,
        to right stewardship of all that God has entrusted
            to us,
        to the way of peace, loving enemies
            and practicing justice,
        to deeds of compassion and reconciliation
            in holiness of life.

We are the people of God,
        gathering to worship the one true God, who is
            three-in-one.
We are God's holy nation,
        giving our allegiance to Jesus Christ as Lord of lords,
        living now according to the pattern of God's future.
We place our hope in the reign of God and its fulfillment,
        in the resurrection of the dead,
        in God's final victory over evil,

and in that day when Christ will come again
    in glory and judgment
to gather his church to reign with him
    in righteousness and peace.
To God be glory in the church and in Christ Jesus
to all generations forever and ever! Amen!

Scripture Index

References to the Scriptures used in the texts of the Article and Commentary sections of the *Confession of Faith in a Mennonite Perspective* are found in this index.

Biblical texts included in the Article section are preceded with an A followed by the number of the article in which it appears, for example Exodus 3:13-14 A-1.

References carried in the Commentary section are preceded with a C followed by the number of the article in which it appears, for example John 10:30 C-1.

Old Testament

Genesis
1 C-5
1–11 A-22
1:1 A-5
1:2 C-3
1:26-27 A-6, C-6
1:26-28 A-21, C-6
1:26-30 A-6
1:31 A-5, A-6
2:15 C-6
2:15-17 C-6
2:17 A-7
2:18 C-6
2:18-23 A-6
2:23-25 C-19
3:1 C-7
3:14-19 C-7
3:16 C-6
3:17 C-7

3:22-24 A-7
4:3-16 C-7
4:15 C-5
6:11-12 A-7
6:11-13 C-7
8:21-22 C-5
9:8-17 A-5
11:1-9 C-7
12:1-3 A-19
12:2-3 A-1
19–20 C-6

Exodus
3:13-14 A-1
6–16 C-5
7:6 C-9
10:1 C-11
12 C-12
13:9 C-11

14:13-14 C-22
15 C-8
15:8 A-24
19:6 C-9
20:1 A-4, C-4
20:1-6 A-1
20:1-17 A-8
20:4-6 A-1
20:8-11 A-21, C-6
20:12 A-19
20:14 A-19, C-19
29:29 C-2
29:35 A-15
31:13 C-11
34:5-7 A-1

Leviticus
8–10 C-16
14:1-9 C-11

New Testament

About the Mennonites

For more information about the Mennonites contact:

Mennonite Church Canada
office@mennonitechurch.ca
www.mennonitechurch.ca
600 Shaftesbury Blvd.
Winnipeg, MB R3P 0M4
Telephone: 204-888-6781
Toll Free: 1-866-888-6785 (North America)
Fax: 204-831-5675

Mennonite Church USA
Mennonite Church USA Executive Board
info@mennoniteusa.org,
www.mennoniteusa.org
Toll-free 1-866-866-2872

Great Plains office
722 Main St., PO Box 347
Newton, KS 67114-0347
Tel: 316-283-5100
Fax: 316-283-0454

Great Lakes office
500 S. Main St., PO Box 1245
Elkhart, IN 46515-1245
Tel: 574-294-7523
Fax: 574-293-1892

www.mennonitechurchusa.org
www.thirdway.com

Additional Resources about the Mennonites

For more copies of this confession as well as books, magazines, and other resources about Mennonites, contact:

Faith & Life Resources
flr@mph.org
718 Main St.
P.O. Box 347
Newton, KS 67114-0347
Tel.: 316-283-5100
Fax: 316-283-0454

Faith & Life Order Line
(Canada and U.S.)
800-743-2484

Herald Press
hp@mph.org
616 Walnut Ave.
Scottdale, PA 15683-1999
Tel.: 724-887-8500
Fax: 724-887-3111

Herald Press Canada
hpcan@mph.org
490 Dutton Dr. Unit C8
Waterloo, ON N2L 6H7
Tel.: 519-747-5722
Fax: 519-747-5721

Herald Press Order Line
(Canada and U.S.)
800-245-7894

Provident Bookstores
Order Line
(Canada and U.S.)
pbsorder@mph.org
Fax: 717-397-8299